DISCARD

7/99

The Reality of Appearance

THE TROMPE L'ŒIL TRADITION IN AMERICAN PAINTING

By Alfred Frankenstein

PUBLISHED BY NEW YORK GRAPHIC SOCIETY LTD.
for an exhibition organized by
UNIVERSITY ART MUSEUM, BERKELEY
in conjunction with
NATIONAL GALLERY OF ART
WHITNEY MUSEUM OF AMERICAN ART
CALIFORNIA PALACE OF THE LEGION OF HONOR
THE DETROIT INSTITUTE OF ARTS

SCHEDULE OF THE EXHIBITION

National Gallery of Art, Washington, D.C.
   March 21–May 3, 1970

Whitney Museum of American Art, New York
   May 19–July 5, 1970

University Art Museum, Berkeley (and)
California Palace of the Legion of Honor, San Francisco
   July 15–August 31, 1970

The Detroit Institute of Arts
   September 15–October 31, 1970

Standard Book Number: 8212–0357–6
Library of Congress Catalog Card Number: 78–104385
Design by Joseph Bourke Del Valle

LIST OF ARTISTS AND WORKS

ACKNOWLEDGMENTS

This first major museum exhibition of American *trompe l'œil* painting has been conceived and organized by Alfred Frankenstein, and I want to express the Museum's gratitude to him for the time and intense energy he has devoted to this job in his capacity as Guest Director of the Exhibition. Without his interest, scholarship, and continued enthusiasm, we would most certainly not have been able to assemble the outstanding exhibition and accompanying publication which we are now able to present.

I would also like to thank Brenda Richardson, Associate Curator, and Susan Rannells, Assistant Curator—both of the University Art Museum staff—who so ably assisted Mr. Frankenstein in all aspects of the organization of the show and preparation of this catalogue.

Our special gratitude is due Forrest Selvig of New York Graphic Society for his careful and cooperative supervision of the publication and distribution of this book.

Many individuals extended themselves far beyond the call of duty in order to assist and enlighten Alfred Frankenstein in the initial stages of his work, and their cooperative attitudes contributed much toward the success of this exhibition. Among these people we especially want to thank Stuart P. Feld, Hirschl and Adler Galleries, New York; Lawrence Fleischman, Kennedy Galleries, Inc., New York; and John K. Howat, Curator of American Painting, The Metropolitan Museum of Art.

I also want to thank the staff members of the respective museums participating in the national circulation of this show. The high caliber of the participating institutions and the interest and cooperation of their individual staff members have assured us a wide audience for this outstanding exhibition.

Most of all, of course, we wish to express our indebtedness to the many lenders who so willingly gave up their paintings for the duration of this exhibition's tour. (A complete listing of the lenders can be found on p. 154 of the present book.) Without their cooperation, there could obviously have been no exhibition at all.

Peter Selz, Director
University Art Museum, Berkeley

Like old soldiers, folktales never die. Unlike old soldiers, however, they never fade away. They are perennially reborn in fresh disguises. They persist as miraculously as the human race itself.

We turn to Book 35 of the *Natural History* by Pliny the Elder. This was completed in the year 77 of the Christian era, but the passage in question deals with painting in Athens in the fifth century B.C.:

Parrhasios, it is recorded, entered into a competition with Zeuxis, who produced a picture of grapes so successfully represented that birds flew up to the stage buildings [in the theater, which served at that time as a public art gallery]; whereupon Parrhasios himself produced such a realistic picture of a curtain that Zeuxis, proud of the verdict of the birds, requested that the curtain should now be drawn and the picture displayed; and when he realized his mistake, with a modesty that did him honor he yielded up the prize, saying that whereas he had deceived birds, Parrhasios had deceived him, an artist.[1]

We turn next to an undated clipping from the New York newspaper known as the *Mail and Express*, which was published between 1880 and 1904. The author of this story had been visiting an unnamed painter in his studio, and there he had seen:

…an ordinary drawing board, eloquent of long and hard usage. There were pencil sketches on it. Three or four cancelled stamps were stuck here and there, and a photograph of an actress, such as is given away with a package of cigarettes, ornamented a corner of the board. Someone had cut his initials into it, and the knife had not been very sharp; and someone else had struck a match across it.

The artist then told the reporter that he proposed to paint an exact copy of that drawing board, and when he finished, he was going to paint the things on the other side. The writer then stepped to the board, turned it around, and discovered— you've guessed it—that it was no drawing board at all, but a painting.[2]

These two stories are identical in plot. They are, in fact, the same folktale, although in the telling they take on trappings separated by twenty-five hundred years—but they contain a considerably deeper meaning than that of their plot alone. Visualize the curtain of Parrhasios: a flat, painted plane with puckers of the gathered cloth seeming to protrude in low relief. Visualize the drawing board which the *Mail and Express* man saw: a flat, painted plane with flat things on it— pencil sketches, canceled stamps, a photograph. Whether in the Athens of Pericles or the New York of William McKinley, realistic deception in painting depends on flatness. Nothing in a truly deceptive painting comes farther forward than the shallow folds of a curtain; more significantly, nothing goes deeper than initials whittled with a dull knife or the scratch of a match across the surface of wood.

There are excellent reasons for this.

Our perception of depth in nature depends upon two types of experience. One is the constant adjustment and readjustment of the muscles of our eyes as we focus upon objects now near, now far, now in the middle ground. The other is binocular parallax, the phenomenon whereby, as one rides in a train, the landscape near at hand moves backward while the landscape at a distance moves in the opposite direction, but more slowly. To draw an example from domestic surroundings—as I look at the ink bottle on my desk and move my head to the left, the bottle moves rightward, but the books standing behind it move along with me. If I stand up and step toward my table, the objects at its edge move downward, while the far edge of the table and everything on it rise straight up in the air. If our eyes alone can be believed, the world around us contains nothing even slightly stable; it is perpetually reeling, collapsing, and moving off in all directions at once.

But muscular adjustment and binocular parallax play no part in our perception of depth in painting. The rock in the foreground and the mountain in the far distance of a painted landscape command exactly the same muscular adjustment because both exist as shapes on the same plane. In perceiving them, we do not change the focus of our eyes from near to far, as we should in perceiving such things in nature; and the absence of these changes in focus tells us, however subtly, that we are not confronted with natural reality.

The absence of binocular parallax plays a much more significant role, however, than the absence of muscular adjustment in aiding us to distinguish between reality and illusion in our visual experiences. The objects represented in a painting are frozen in their mutual relationships; they never change their relationship to each other when we move, as objects in nature constantly do, and our failure to perceive such changes in relationship informs us that we are in the presence of a representation of external reality, not of external reality itself.

If, however, depth in painting is removed or very greatly reduced, then the eye may be fooled into mistaking a painted thing for a real thing. The muscular adjustment required to change the focus of the eye from a fold to the flat of a curtain is very slight, and scarcely any binocular parallax can be observed between the edge of a photograph and the board to which it is pasted. Paint such things and the illusion of reality may be attained, at least for a moment. The momentariness of the illusion is extremely important. Our pleasure in *trompe l'œil* arises from the realization that our *œil* has been *trompe*'d.

This, then, must be the first rule of the game for the artist who wishes to fool the eye of the spectator: Choose objects, situations, and compositional devices involving as little depth as possible. Wherefore now arises the pictorial convention whereby a flat, broad, unyielding surface— a door, a wall, or, in Greek and Roman mosaics, a floor— stops the eye at the picture plane, while objects placed upon this flat, broad, unyielding surface seem to protrude—but never very far—into the spectator's space.

Another aspect of *trompe l'œil* can be more quickly defined. That is the aspect of scale. The eye is not likely to be fooled by a representation much larger or smaller than the size in which the represented object is seen in normal experience. A *trompe l'œil* painting of Westminster Abbey or Niagara Falls is unthinkable. That is why *trompe l'œil* is almost entirely a department of still life. Still life deals with objects small enough to be represented in their natural size on a canvas of manageable proportions.

That, however, is not quite all there is to the question. We return for a moment to Pliny and the sequel to his story of Zeuxis and Parrhasios:

It is said that Zeuxis subsequently painted a child carrying grapes, and when birds flew to the fruit with the same frankness as before, he strode up to the picture in anger with it and said, "I have painted the grapes better than the child; if I had made a success of the child, the birds would inevitably have been afraid of it."

Zeuxis was wrong. Figures of living beings, human or animal, do not lend themselves well to *trompe l'œil*, no doubt because we are used to seeing them constantly in motion. Motion is of their essence. They can be represented in painting with marvelous success, but not in *trompe l'œil* painting; the eye can often be fooled by the jewels and costumes in portraits by Holbein, but not by the faces and hands. It is no accident at all that dead animals are favorite subjects for *trompe l'œil*, but very seldom live ones, and then invariably *tiny* live ones; the fly is proverbially part of the *trompe l'œil* tradition (although it is actually far less important to that tradition than it is proverbially supposed to be). In general, *trompe l'œil* insists upon subjects that stay put in nature as they do in art. In the last analysis, it should cause little surprise that still lifes are very likely to be still.

Despite its subtitle, the current exhibition does not consist exclusively of *trompe l'œil* painting as we have defined it here. In the nature of things, it could not be restricted in that way. Art styles are never consistently practiced in accordance with their textbook definitions. There were four great still-life painters in the United States in the nineteenth century, and this exhibition is organized around representative samplings of their work. The earliest of the four, Raphaelle Peale, practiced textbook *trompe l'œil* very little; of the six Raphaelle Peales in the present exhibition, only one, *A Deception*, is strictly and totally in the *trompe l'œil* manner. On the other hand, the last of our four major figures, John Haberle, practiced almost nothing but orthodox *trompe l'œil*. Of the eleven Haberles assembled here, only one, *A Dishpan of Flowers*, does not involve some device to stop the eye at the picture plane. Our other two giants, William Michael Harnett and John Frederick Peto, divide their attention about equally between strict *trompe l'œil* painting and still-life painting of a more conventional kind.

However, the conventional still-life painting of all these men is strongly conditioned by attitudes and devices derived from or related to *trompe l'œil*. What is commonly called a tabletop, in the still lifes of Raphaelle Peale looks far more often like a narrow shelf or ledge, placed parallel to the picture plane. This commits the artist to as little depth as possible, and the objects on that tabletop, shelf, or ledge are placed as close to its forward edge as they can be with comfort to themselves and to the spectator's sensibilities. Raphaelle Peale very definitely dislikes deep space. The same thing is true of Harnett and Peto, who came from Peale's city of Philadelphia and were formed by his example; but with these artists objects often dangle over the table's edge, and in some early works of Harnett a knife, pen, or matchstick may break right through the picture plane to be molded in a naïve relief of built-up paint on the spectator's side of the frame.

Raphaelle Peale is deeply concerned with the rendering of textures and with subtly observed highlights and reflections in the surfaces of metals, glass, and glazed ceramics. The same thing is true of Harnett; but it is not at all true of Peto, who casts the same soft, radiant texture over everything he paints.

The relatively heavy representation given to Harnett in the present show does not reflect a predilection for him on the part of the exhibition's organizer; it arises, rather, from a number of objective circumstances: There are more surviving works by Harnett than by any of the others; he used a greater variety of subjects and approaches than anybody else; and his highly systematic turn of mind, wherein he was unique among the American still-life painters of his time, makes it possible to perceive in the sequence of his works a developing personality such as no other American still-life painter reveals. Furthermore, Harnett was by far the most influential still-life painter who ever lived in this country. Specific details about all the artists in this show can be found in the comments on their pictures on subsequent pages of this book.

Besides its four main personalities, the present exhibition provides examples of many lesser figures of nineteenth-century American still life in or related to the *trompe l'œil* tradition. Some of these lesser artists are little known; a few, indeed, are being brought before the general public for the first time on this occasion. Nineteenth-century American still life totally devoid of relationship to *trompe l'œil*, such as the work of Sargent or Chase or Emil Carlsen, forms no part of the present show, not because we don't like these artists, but because they listened to a different drum from the one we happen to be beating.

The earliest surviving still lifes were known in their day as *rhyparography*, literally *garbage pictures*. They are mosaics from the floors of Greek and Roman houses, and they represent the fallout from a meal: fruit skins, nutshells, bones, chicken claws, and all such, often depicted with mice and cockroaches in attendance. Since antiquity, then, still life has been associated with the dining room and with general mess and disorder In Harnett's world of overturned inkwells, scattered ashes and crumbs, and incandescent dottles from overturned pipes burning holes in newspapers there may be more reflection of un-still life than still life is supposed to provide; and the same may be true of Peto's tattered books, torn papers, and debris of every imaginable kind. But if there is one thing more tiresome than the criticism of still life for its alleged failure to deal with great issues— a criticism that was brought against it throughout the period of the current show—it is the effort to raise the standing of the subject by discovering that it does, after all, deal with profoundly earnest matters.

The heyday of American still-life painting was the last quarter of the nineteenth century; sixteen of the twenty-seven artists represented in this exhibition were of that era. The twenty-seven fall quite naturally into four groups: those artists, eleven in all, whose period of major activity came before 1870; then the three giants, Harnett, Peto, and Haberle; then ten lesser painters strongly influenced by Harnett; finally, three lesser painters at the end of the century (Alexander, Ramsey, and Yates) who successfully resisted the domination of Harnett and his ideas. The catalogue is arranged in accordance with these groups.

1. *Plinii Naturalis Historiae*, translated by H. Rackham (Cambridge and London), n.d., vol. IX, pp. 309–311.
2. Alfred Frankenstein, *After the Hunt*, Berkeley and Los Angeles: University of California Press, 1969, second edition, p. 121. This remarkable book is indispensable, especially to the writer of this catalogue.

COLOR PLATES

16   Goodes, *Fishbowl Fantasy*, page 52.

13

20   Harnett, *Fruit and Asparagus*, page 58.

15

50 Harnett, *Golden Horseshoe*, page 84.

64   Peto, *Old Companions*, page 104.

83   Goodwin, *Hunting Cabin Door*, page 128.

88   Pope, *The Trumpeter Swan*, page 134.

89   Elmer, *Magic Glasses*, page 136 (not in exhibition).

CATALOGUE OF THE EXHIBITION

Dimensions are in inches, height preceding width. Dates enclosed in parentheses do not appear on works. All works are included in all showings of the exhibition, with the following exceptions: catalogue #28, Washington and New York only; catalogue #37, Washington, New York and California only; catalogue #43 and #60, New York and California only; catalogue #44, not in exhibition; catalogue #46, San Francisco only; and catalogue #89, not in exhibition.

JAMES PEALE
1749—1831

1   James Peale, *Still Life*, n.d. Oil on panel, $18^3/_4 \times 25^3/_4$.
M. H. de Young Memorial Museum, San Francisco.

James Peale, brother of the celebrated Charles Willson Peale, and uncle of Raphaelle and Rubens Peale, who are also represented in the current exhibition, divided his attention about equally between portraits, miniatures, and still lifes. He may therefore be regarded as the founding father of the Philadelphia still-life tradition. Four daughters and a son of James Peale all painted still lifes, and they carried the tradition down to the late nineteenth century and the era of Harnett and Peto.

I

RAPHAELLE PEALE
1774-1825

2   Raphaelle Peale, *A Deception*, 1802(?). India ink and pencil on paper, $16 \times 10^3/_4$.
Courtesy of Kennedy Galleries, Inc., New York.

The New-York Historical Society's Dictionary of Artists in America lists seventeen painters bearing the name of Peale, including James, his brother Charles Willson, and fifteen of their descendants. This does not exhaust the list, however, since there were other painters in the family who bore different surnames, like Charles Peale Polk. There were so many painting Peales in Philadelphia at one time that the name became synonymous with "painter" in that city and its environs, just as "Bach" was synonymous with "musician" in eighteenth-century Saxony.

The patriarchal Charles Willson Peale—scientist, inventor, portrait painter, founder of the first science museum and the first art school in the United States—was the most important member of the tribe. He married three times and had seventeen children, all of whom he named after artists and scientists—Raphaelle, Rembrandt, Rubens, Titian, Angelica Kaufmann, Linnaeus, and so on—and some of these children grew up to be distinguished painters and scientists in their own right.

Raphaelle, oldest son of Charles Willson Peale, is—at least from the point of view of contemporary taste—the most important of Charles Willson's artistic children. He assisted in the management of the family museum, painted portraits, and cut silhouettes, but his principal claim to glory lies in his still lifes; he is the first really distinguished still-life specialist to emerge in this country, and he is one of the four major still-life painters of the nineteenth century in the United States. Most of his still lifes were painted after 1800.

A Deception (a word widely used in England and America before the fancier term *trompe l'œil* drove it out) employs the old convention of the card rack—strips of ribbon or tape under whose tension various papers are held in place on a flat surface. This convention reached its climax in the work of William Michael Harnett and John Frederick Peto in the 1880's. The picture bears on its back a curious inscription, stating that it was created by Raphaelle Peale in 1802, and tracing its history among his descendants for a hundred years.

In contemplating a picture of this kind, one is tempted to seek some anecdotal connection between the objects represented, but this line of inquiry is almost invariably disappointing. Edward Penington, the Philadelphia merchant and political figure whose name appears on a kind of seal toward the bottom of the picture, had died in 1796; next to it, however, is a prospectus for one of the innumerable publishing ventures of Mathew Carey, Philadelphia's leading bookman, dated 1802. (Apparently Carey did not get enough subscriptions to bring out his "Complete System of Biography"; at all events, he says nothing about it in his autobiography.)

A Deception contains tickets for public entertainments of various kinds, including a Washington's Birthday ball; there is also a ticket representing a curtain hung between two trees, with exotic birds and reptiles roundabout. It is inscribed as follows:

The Beasts will teach thee!
Admit the Bearer to
PEALE'S MUSEUM
Containing the wonderful works of
NATURE!
Equal to 25 Cents

2

3   Raphaelle Peale, *Still Life with Red Pepper*, (ca. 1810). Oil on panel, 11³/₄ × 15.
      Wadsworth Atheneum, Hartford, Connecticut: The Ella Gallup Sumner and Mary Catlin Sumner Collection.

The corner of the tabletop thrusting into deep space is most unusual for Raphaelle Peale. Even more unusual is the realistically inexplicable descending wedge of light in the background, which turns the red pepper into the head of a rocket. The

Wadsworth Atheneum dates this painting ca. 1810, but Edward H. Dwight (in *The Peale Family*, exhibition catalogue, The Detroit Institute of Arts, 1967) dates it ca. 1817.

4   Raphaelle Peale, *Still Life with Steak*, (ca. 1817). Oil on panel, 13³/₈ × 19¹/₂.
      Munson-Williams-Proctor Institute, Utica, New York.

The Dutch inspiration of Raphaelle Peale's still-life style is more forcefully suggested here than in other Peales of the present show. The picture reminds one of the heaped-up meats and vegetables of a Frans Snyders, but in an exceedingly moderate, not to say puritanically limited measure. It is interesting to see that in America, the land of plenty, in its century of opulence, the only still-

life painter to rival the materialistic extravagance of the seventeenth-century Dutch was the German immigrant, Severin Roesen. Raphaelle's balancing of the green of the cabbage against three reds (steak, carrots, beet) is decidedly worthy of note here. Is the raw flesh nothing more than meat for the broiler?

3

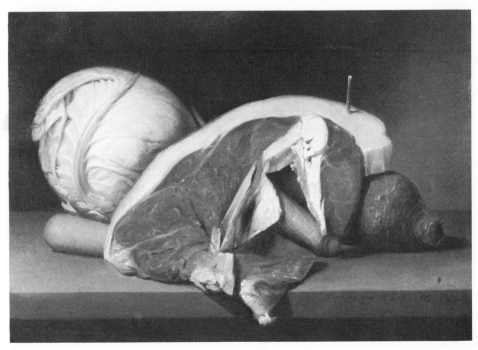

4

5   Raphaelle Peale, *Still Life with Dried Fish*, 1815. Oil on panel, $10^1/_8 \times 15$.
Historical Society of Pennsylvania, Philadelphia.

Harnett's contrasted textures are strikingly predicted here, or, to state the case more accurately, Harnett in his time will go back to the contrasted textures of Raphaelle Peale, of which this is an especially good example: the smoothness of porcelain versus the roughness of stoneware, the papery outer peel of the dried onion versus the succulence of the fresh one, and the crinkly texture of the fish's skin versus everything. The composition, with its five varieties of roundness and its long swoop of fish binding the rondures together, suggests why many critics draw parallels between the American still-life painters of the nineteenth century and the geometric-abstract painters of the twentieth.

6   Raphaelle Peale. *Lemons and Sugar*, (ca. 1822). Oil on panel, $12^3/_4 \times 15^7/_8$.
The Reading Public Museum and Art Gallery, Reading, Pennsylvania.

Perforated ceramic baskets of one kind and another are almost a Peale trademark. So are the reflections in glazed and metal surfaces which appear here. The picture is signed "R. Peale, 1847," but since Raphaelle Peale died in 1825, this inscription is of somewhat dubious authenticity.

7   Raphaelle Peale, *Still Life with Strawberries*, 1822. Oil on canvas, 16×22.
Collection Mr. and Mrs. Robert C. Graham, New York.

Carlyle Burroughs once observed that John Frederick Peto confers a curious kind of animation on the objects in his paintings and thereby turns still life into a species of genre. The same thing is true of Raphaelle Peale as exemplified here. The painting is also a study in ten kinds of roundness— sugar bowl, sauce dishes, glass container, strawberries, nut bowl, hazelnuts, almonds, raisins, orange, and cream pitcher; furthermore, it is a study in almost as many different textures.

5

6

7

RUBENS PEALE
1784–1865

8   Rubens Peale, *From Nature in the Garden*, n.d. Oil on canvas, 20 × 24.
Courtesy of Kennedy Galleries, Inc., New York.

9   Rubens Peale, *Magpie Eating Cake*, 1865. Oil on canvas, 19 × 27.
Courtesy of Kennedy Galleries, Inc., New York.

Rubens Peale, fourth son of Charles Willson Peale, spent most of his life managing museums, first for his father in Philadelphia, then for his brother Rembrandt in Baltimore, finally on his own in New York. He did not begin to paint until he had retired from museum management at the age of seventy-one. His painting is primitive and whimsical in style. He particularly liked to paint birds in landscape and birds in still-life arrangements, but *live* birds; the hanging-game picture was not for him. *Partridge Piece, Happy Family*, is a characteristic and revealing Rubens Peale title.

The staring uniformity of emphasis on all the objects in *From Nature in the Garden* is the sign manual of the primitive painter. So is the precise bilateral symmetry of the composition. *Magpie Eating Cake* is full of odd, amusing touches in drawing. Note particularly the almost cubistic, Picasso-like wineglass.

8

9

10   Charles Bird King, *Still Life, Game,* 1806. Oil on canvas, 11 × 14.
Hirschl and Adler Galleries, Inc., New York.

It would be a rash man who would say this is the earliest known American still life of dead game, but it is the earliest work of that kind—ultimately to become so excessively common as to constitute a public nuisance—known to the compiler of this catalogue. Its date indicates that it was painted in England, when King was studying with Benjamin West.

Charles Bird King was born in Newport, Rhode Island. He was with West in London from 1805 to 1812, and finally settled in Washington, D.C., where he achieved considerable celebrity, especially as a painter of the Indian chiefs who frequently came to the capital on behalf of their tribes. His present celebrity, however, is based very largely on a single still life, known as *The Vanity of an Artist's Dream,* that was unfortunately not available for this exhibition. It represents dusty, dilapidated books, brushes, a palette, a fragment of classic sculpture, stale food, and other sweepings of an artist's studio, all thrown helter-skelter into a niche, or closet, with notice of a sheriff's sale tacked alongside it. Our picture—with its dark tone, its crepuscular space behind the game, and its high, severe windows—has a melancholy, charnel-house atmosphere similar to that of *The Vanity of an Artist's Dream* and very much in keeping with the general romantic mood of the period.

10

JOHN F. FRANCIS
1808–1886

11 John F. Francis, *Still Life with Apples*, n.d. Oil on canvas, 25 × 30.
Collection Barbara B. Lassiter, Winston-Salem, North Carolina.

John F. Francis was born in Philadelphia, apparently lived there during his childhood, but spent all of his mature life in small towns of central and eastern Pennsylvania. He died in Jeffersonville, Pennsylvania, where he resided for the last two decades of his life.

Well over half of Francis's known work is in the department of still life, and nearly all of that has to do with dessert—fruit, cake, nuts, wine, cider, and the baskets, pitchers, glasses, and table implements that go with them. He exploits the smallest repertoire of any American still-life painter whose work one can study in any degree of detail. His relationship to the *trompe l'œil* tradition is a bit tenuous, but his modeling of objects, like the apples in this picture, can be as powerful as the modeling of a Raphaelle Peale or a Harnett, and he is one of the major links between these two. His color, as Wolfgang Born once noted, is full of "novel shades of pink, blue, green, and yellow." In this he smacks a bit of impressionism, and his blond, high-keyed palette always provides one of the most distinctive accents in a general exhibition of American still life.

II

SEVERIN ROESEN
Dates of birth and death unknown

12 Severin Roesen, *Fruit with Bird's Nest*, n.d. Oil on canvas, 33 × 39.
Collection Dick Button, New York.

Nature's bounty is a main theme in American literature and American landscape painting of the nineteenth century, but it is very little celebrated in the American still life of the same period, and then mostly in the work of Roesen. About 1848, he came here from Germany, where he had been a painter of porcelain and enamels. He lived and exhibited in New York from 1850 to 1857, but he seems to have spent most of his American years in Williamsport, Pennsylvania, where he arrived around 1858 and from which he disappeared around 1871. Nothing more is known about him. The tale that he died in a Philadelphia poorhouse cannot be substantiated.

Richard B. Stone, who in 1951 published *A Study of the Williamsport Painter, S. Roesen* (Lycoming County Historical Society), listed 136 paintings by Roesen, all but two of them extravagantly heaped-up still lifes of flowers or fruit, and all of them in a somewhat naïvely detailed style. He frequently uses two marble ledges to support his flowers or fruits, as he does here, and he frequently associates his fruits with drinkables and the glassware to go with them. He loves the calligraphy of vine tendrils and often bends them into his signature, as in this example.

12

13 Martin Johnson Heade, *A Vase of Corn Lilies and Heliotrope,* 1863. Oil on canvas, $16^3/_8 \times 12^3/_8$.
City Art Museum of Saint Louis, Museum Purchase, Eliza McMillan Fund.

Heade, painter of landscape, portraits, still life, and Brazilian hummingbirds, was born in Pennsylvania, studied in Europe, and was the most restless wanderer among the major American artists of his period; there was scarcely any part of the Western Hemisphere with which he was not familiar, although he stayed put in St. Augustine, Florida, for the last nineteen years of his life.

Heade painted flower still lifes of several kinds, but the best of them are those in which, Peale-like, he places his objects on a very narrow ledge against a background of empty colored space, with a single vase of very striking silhouette in dead center. He shows a subtle painterliness in the handling of objects that is quite unknown to any of the artists who follow the *trompe l'œil* tradition more strictly.

13

14 Voltaire Combe, *Butterflies*, (1863). Two watercolors on paper (framed together), each $11^5/_{16} \times 9^1/_4$. Onondaga Historical Association, Syracuse, New York.

Scientific illustration is an important department of *trompe l'œil*; John James Audubon was to some degree a *trompe l'œil* painter. In the present show we are able to touch only momentarily on the subject of scientific illustration, and we prefer to do so with a work by a little-known artist who has not hitherto been represented in an exhibition of national scope.

Voltaire Combe was a Character with a capital C. His parents' surname was Combs. They saddled him with the curious given name of Captain, which proved to be an embarrassment to him when he served as a sergeant in the Civil War. No wonder he threw it all overboard, emerging first as Raphael Combe and then as Voltaire. From Raphael to Voltaire is a pilgrim's progress indeed.

Combe, who came from Jordan, New York, began his career in Syracuse, painting the elaborately decorated window shades which were widely employed in commercial establishments in mid-century. After the Civil War, Combe moved to New York City where, among other things, he did much work for Currier and Ives. He spent the last years of his life in Michigan, and was painting literary and genre scenes as late as 1912.

Butterflies comes from a sketchbook, full of camp scenes and nature study, which Combe carried with him during the Civil War. He was not, strictly speaking, a scientific illustrator, but his nature sketches are indicative of a wide-ranging curiosity that was an important part of his make-up. He is one of the many rewarding American artists of the nineteenth century who have never been studied or even cursorily explored.

We should like to acknowledge our indebtedness, so far as Combe is concerned, to Richard Wright of the Onondaga Historical Association, who brought up his name in the course of conversation regarding the next artist we turn to.

S. E. HARLOW
Dates of birth and death unknown

15 S. E. Harlow, *Mrs. Redfield's Socks*, n.d. Oil on canvas, $15^3/_8 \times 11^1/_4$.
Onondaga Historical Association, Syracuse, New York.

Trompe l'œil breeds more verbal folklore than painting of any other kind, and it is particularly fitting that a folk painting like *Mrs. Redfield's Socks* should produce one of the most characteristic of these stories.

This picture bears on its back the following inscription: "Present to Mrs. Redfield by S. E. Harlow." No one knows who S. E. Harlow may have been, but Amy Redfield, in Richard G. Case's phrase, "...was a ferocious and proud knitter." She turned out innumerable pairs of socks for Civil War soldiers even though, according to family tradition, she was going blind from cataracts. The painting is supposed to have been sent to Mrs. Redfield by one of the recipients of her socks to tell her, in a nice way, that their white tops were not of the same size.

The picture is recorded for the first time in the collection of the Onondaga Historical Association in 1911. The magazine in which Mr. Case told its story is called the *New York Folk Lore Quarterly* (June 1967), not, be it well noted, *New York History*.

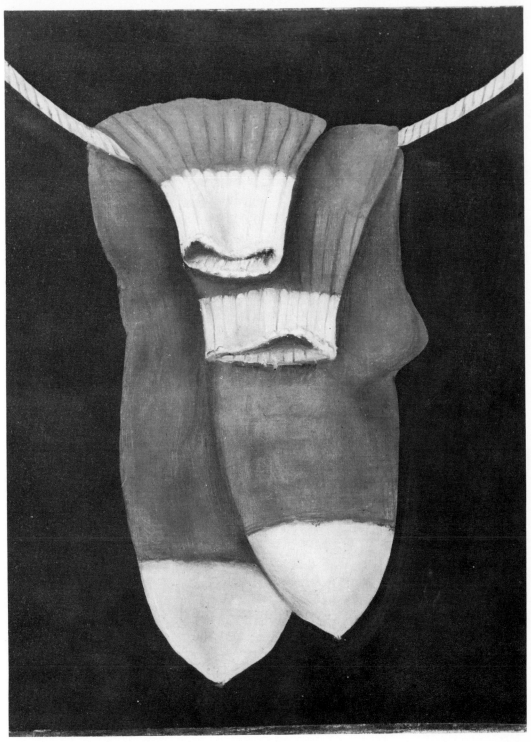

15

EDWARD A. GOODES
Dates of birth and death unknown

16 Edward A. Goodes, *Fishbowl Fantasy*, 1867. Oil on canvas, 30 × 25¹/₈.
Hirschl and Adler Galleries, Inc., New York.

It is incredible that a painter who has mastered so fantastic and unforgettable a style as the one displayed here should be all but totally unknown. Goodes is recorded as having participated in the annual exhibitions at the Pennsylvania Academy of the Fine Arts between 1855 and 1868, and a still life by him, dated 1887, has recently turned up on the New York market. That is the full extent of his biography so far as it is known at present.

Fishbowl Fantasy may be an isolated freak in the work of Goodes; we do not know enough about it to say. Its microscopically detailed, unfocused examination of minutiae should place it in the folksy tradition of Rubens Peale, but it doesn't; the picture looks forward, rather, to surrealism and to the particular brand of it practiced by Ivan Albright.

16

WILLIAM M. DAVIS.
1829–1920

17 William M. Davis, *A Canvas Back*, n.d. Oil on canvas, $8^1/_4 \times 10^1/_4$.
Melville Collection, Suffolk Museum and Carriage House, Stony Brook, Long Island.

William M. Davis lived all his long life in the village of Port Jefferson, Long Island. He had some contact with the celebrated genre painter William Sidney Mount, who lived in the nearby town of Stony Brook, and whose work he occasionally imitated. He is usually dismissed as a mere follower of Mount, but that is incorrect.

A Canvas Back precisely materializes the legend of Zeuxis and Parrhasios as recounted by Pliny the Elder and repeated in the Foreword. Davis may have read Pliny, but it is much more likely that his picture is an oil-on-canvas version of the folktale which, if Pliny can be believed, was half a millennium old when he told it. Precisely the same idea is embodied in John Frederick Peto's *Lincoln and the Pfleger Stretcher* (#59 of the present catalogue). The idea, of course, is to make the spectator think he is contemplating the back of a canvas—that the painting he really wants to see is on the other side.

The brown-rose stamp on the lower of the two letters in the Davis painting was issued on August 18, 1861. The green stamp at the wrong end of the upper letter (which is addressed to Davis at Port Jefferson and contains paper money) came out on April 12, 1870. The use of stamps of such widely separated issues suggests that Davis was not drawing his models from his current mail and therefore that he may have been trying to make the painting look older than it actually is. Davis was twenty-eight years older than Peto, but he outlived the master of Island Heights by more than a decade. *A Canvas Back*, with its bank note, its postage stamps, and its Parrhasian trickery, has very much the feeling of the Harnett-Peto period. If it was painted not much later than its later stamp—*i.e.*, around 1870—it anticipates the devices of the Harnett-Peto era and indicates that they are older than they have generally been thought to be.

17

WILLIAM MICHAEL HARNETT
1848(?)–1892

Harnett is the central figure in American still life, whether of the *trompe l'œil* or any other tradition. Two-thirds of his work is lost; even so, infinitely more of it has been preserved than of the work of any other artist represented in this exhibition. He had his personal eccentricities, but he had a tidy mind, and it is possible to perceive the development of his style from year to year, and at times from month to month; this cannot be said of any other American still-life painter. He was enormously influential in his own time, and the widespread reflection of his ideas in the work of others clearly makes him the *chef d'école*.

Harnett's career lasted only eighteen years and divides itself, with typical Harnettian neatness, into three six-year periods: from 1874, when he began to paint in oil, to 1880, when he went to Europe, these six years having been spent mostly in Philadelphia; 1880 to 1886 in Europe, mostly in Munich; and 1886 to the artist's death in 1892, entirely in New York. Details about his career will be provided in the following notes on the individual works.

18 William M. Harnett, *Dante*, 1873. Bronze medallion mounted on panel, $2^5/_8$ in diameter.
Collection Mrs. Harold H. Hays, Philadelphia.

Harnett's father had been a shoemaker, his brother was a saddler, and two sisters were seamstresses; it was only natural, therefore, for the future painter to start out in the crafts. He began his career as an engraver of fancy designs on table silver, and he learned enough about metalwork to produce this relief, his only known piece of sculpture. One can easily visualize it, slightly reduced, as a medallion set in the broad end of a spoon handle.

19 William M. Harnett, *Dante in His Study*, (1873). Watercolor on paper, $7^3/_4 \times 7^1/_4$.
Collection Mr. and Mrs. Morton Funger, Chevy Chase, Maryland.

For seven year, while working in the silver shops, Harnett studied art in night classes at the Pennsylvania Academy of the Fine Arts and at Cooper Union in New York. The few surviving drawings of this period are mostly after classical casts; this painting, in keeping, is an exact copy of a fresco by Luca Signorelli painted around 1499 in the Cathedral of Orvieto. Harnett's color is identical with Luca's, which means he had access to a good color print of the fresco or another artist's copy of it. American art students of the 1870's are not supposed to have known anything about the old masters, but there is increasing evidence to show that they were not as naïve as we used to think they were.

18

19

20 William M. Harnett, *Fruit and Asparagus*, 1875. Oil on canvas, 18 × 24.
    Collection Mr. and Mrs. Jess Pavey, Birmingham, Michigan.

In the spring of 1875 a painting called *Fruit* was exhibited by Harnett at the National Academy of Design, and his professional career may be dated from that event. *Fruit and Asparagus* looks astonishingly expert for a young man just starting out, but on close examination one can see that Harnett here relies much more on draftsmanship than he will later, that the surface textures of the objects are scarcely differentiated at all, and that the tabletop, although it reveals a corner and so can be read as going back into space at its right-hand end, is still mainly a shelf or ledge in the manner of Raphaelle Peale.

21 William M. Harnett, *Still Life, Basket of Fruit*, 1875. Oil on canvas, 18 × 26¹/₂.
    The Reading Public Museum and Art Gallery, Reading, Pennsylvania.

Raphaelle Peale's still lifes are mostly of edibles, and those of Francis mostly of fruit, so it is not surprising that Harnett emphasizes gastronomic motifs in his early works. The naïvely built-up, three-dimensional nailheads in the basket represent a striving for the literal which Harnett will soon abandon.

20

21

22 William M. Harnett, *Jake's Solace*, 1875. Oil on canvas, 12 × 10.
Collection Mr. and Mrs. Cresson Pugh, Mamaroneck, New York.

23 William M. Harnett, *Jake's Second Solace*, 1877. Oil on canvas, 12 × 10.
Collection William Selnick, New York.

The mug-and-pipe picture may be a Harnett invention; at least before Harnett's time the mug and pipe appear in no American still life known to the present writer. The mug and pipe are seldom associated with food as they are here, but this pair of pictures dramatically illustrates one very important aspect of Harnett's methods: his way of working endless variations on the same subject and the same compositional formula. At first glance, these two paintings seem identical; then one becomes aware of the fact that in one the objects are resting on a packing case and in the other on a table, that there are more matches in one than in the other, that the bread and bologna are not quite in the same position in both, and so on. Harnett made extremely close variations from one still-life arrangement to another, but he never painted an exact replica.

24 William M. Harnett, *Five-Dollar Bill*, 1877. Oil on canvas, 8 × 12¹/₈.
Philadelphia Museum of Art: Alex Simpson, Jr., Collection.

Raphaelle Peale painted a picture (now lost) entitled *A Bill*. If the bill in question was a bank note, it is the earliest bank note in American art of which we have any record; if it was not, then the honor of inaugurating that subject in American painting must be accorded this work by Harnett.

It has repeatedly been suggested that Harnett and his school painted paper money because Americans of their time liked money so much that they had to have pictures of it to worship, but this view completely misses the point. As the Foreword makes clear, *trompe l'œil* depends on flatness, and nothing is flatter than a five-dollar bill, not even a one. The motivation for this type of painting, then, is aesthetic, not sociological.

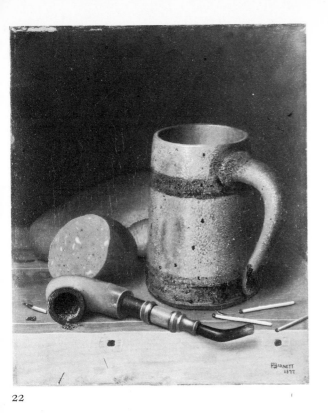

22

23

24

25 William M. Harnett, *Writing Table*, 1877. Oil on canvas, 8 × 12.
Philadelphia Museum of Art: Alex Simpson, Jr., Collection.

In the late 1870's, Harnett produced a considerable series of writing-table still lifes; this motif, in fact, dominates his early work in tandem with the mug and pipe. Nearly all the writing-table pictures contain a folded letter in longhand, always upside down, always tantalizingly legible in part. (If the letter were right side up, it would draw attention to itself too blatantly.) These letters afford us the guilty pleasure of reading someone else's correspondence. The letter here says, "...received you.../early part of last mo.../and was extremely glad/to hear that...u had succe.../ful reflecting..."

26 William M. Harnett, *Still Life*, 1877. Oil on canvas, 11$^1/_2$ × 13$^1/_2$.
Collection Dr. and Mrs. John J. McDonough, Youngstown, Ohio.

The orthodox Harnett mug-and-pipe picture of the 1870's in an especially persuasive example.

27 William M. Harnett, *Job Lot, Cheap*, 1878. Oil on canvas, 18 × 36.
Reynolda House, Winston-Salem, North Carolina.

Harnett begins to hit his stride here. The size is greater than anything he has attempted before, his mastery of varied and contrasted textures is complete, and his composition breaks away from formula to create a unique, unrepeated, individual work, one which so impressed John Frederick Peto that he appropriated both the idea and the title for a painting of his own (see #60 of the present catalogue). Here Harnett begins his practice of teasing one's curiosity with carefully painted labels that cannot be read. This device vaguely suggests surrealism, and the geometry of the books suggests abstraction; it is easy to see why, when Harnett was revived by the Downtown Gallery in 1939, the press treated him as if he were a modern artist who had somehow strayed into the nineteenth century and remained there.

25

26

27

28 William M. Harnett, *Memento Mori—"To This Favour,"* 1879. Oil on canvas, 24 × 32.
The Cleveland Museum of Art, Mr. and Mrs. William H. Marlatt Fund.

The *memento mori*—the still life with a skull as a reminder of death—is an old, widespread motif. It is usually associated with jewels, and the painter usually lavishes more care and attention on these worthless baubles that you can't take with you than on anything else. Harnett gives the theme an appropriately stark, dramatic treatment, with a deeply shadowed arch like the vault of a grave behind the skull, books lying flat as tombstones, a snuffed-out candle, and a quotation from *Hamlet* written on the inside of the loose book-cover that dangles over the edge of the table as precariously as human life on the edge of the abyss: "Now get you to my lady's chamber, and tell her, let her paint an inch thick, to this favour she must come…"

29 William M. Harnett, *The Social Club,* 1879. Oil on canvas, 13 × 20.
Collection Mr. and Mrs. J. William Middendorf II, New York.

The meerschaum pipe with cherrywood stem is Harnett's favorite still-life object in the first period of his career. The briar pipe with a gold collar and band is also a Harnett favorite. Clay pipes recur in a few works. The others are strangers which never appear again.

28

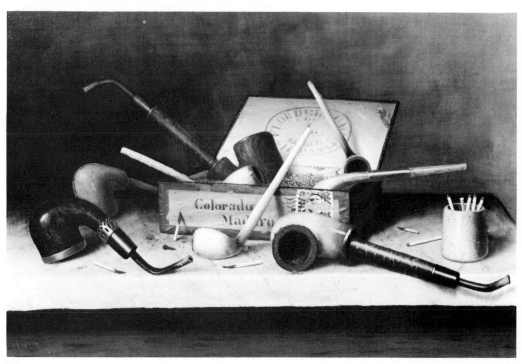

29

30   William M. Harnett, *The Broker's Table*, 1879. Oil on canvas, 9 × 12.
      Collection Mr. and Mrs. Donald S. Stralem, New York.

Another of Harnett's writing-table pictures, this time with a letter that reads: "...p...posed to offer some/further shares for sale,/it is necessary for me to ex-/plain that the sale of these/shares is not urgent al-/though it is desirable because apart from the..."

31   William M. Harnett, *The Secretary's Table*, 1879. Oil on canvas, 14 × 20.
      Preston Morton Collection, Santa Barbara Museum of Art.

A most exceptional variation on the writing-table theme, with unusually brilliant and subtle color, and on the note pad an inscription that might have some autobiographical significance: "June 28/See Mr. Clarke/at St. George Hotel." Thomas B. Clarke was one of the leading collectors of American art at that time.

30

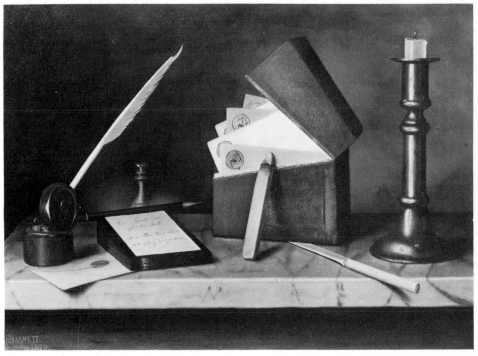

31

32   William M. Harnett, *London Times, April 9, 1880*, 1880. Oil on canvas, $5^7/_8 \times 8^1/_2$.
Private Collection, New York.

33   William M. Harnett, *New York Herald, July 11, 1880*, 1880. Oil on canvas, $5^3/_8 \times 7^1/_8$.
Collection Mrs. Mimi David Bloch, New York.

Harnett went to Europe in January, 1880, and overnight his work took on a new direction. His pictures shrink dramatically in size and his brushmanship acquires a highly distinctive, miniaturistic quality, with a shower of little highlights all over the surface of the canvas and with greater freedom and painterliness than hitherto in the rendering of edges. He tries out this new style in a series of pictures, all involving a tabletop with a gray stoneware jug or beer stein at the right, plus a meerschaum pipe, a book, and a folded newspaper. The newspapers are carefully dated in sequence from early January to July 29, 1880. Ten pictures in this series are known to exist; those in the present show are numbers eight and nine. In the series one can clearly perceive Harnett feeling his way into his new style and painstakingly documenting each step of his progress with the dates on the newspapers.

In several pictures of the series, including the two we present, Harnett turns away from the ambiguous expanse of neutral color which has hitherto served him as background for his tabletop pictures and employs a paneled wall by way of background. He thereby boxes in his shallow space more specifically than heretofore. This boxing-in will shortly become the rule rather than the exception and will be employed by Harnett for the rest of his life. But there is almost invariably a deep, dark recess in the pictures with the paneled background, and it is almost invariably on the right-hand side. Harnett was a very systematic man.

32

33

34 William M. Harnett, *Searching the Scriptures*, 1880. Oil on canvas, 29 × 24¹/₂.
Collection Mrs. Mollie D. Snyder, Philadelphia.

Harnett spent the first half of 1880 in London, then went to Frankfurt with a wealthy gentleman of that city whose name, apparently, was Johann Conrad Cronau. He lived in Cronau's house for six months, and his host bought everything he painted during that time. *Searching the Scriptures* is, in all probability, one of his Frankfurt achievements. It was probably influenced by the costume genre pictures of Meissonier, which were enormously popular all over the world at that time.

Harnett had occasionally painted the human figure before going to Europe, but he seems to have painted it much more frequently abroad than at home. His handling of the human figure is plausible enough and occasionally brilliant, but in this work his predilection for still life gets the better of him. The great things here are the icy silver inkwell, the warm copper candlestick with its stub of translucent candle, the books on table and floor, and the quill pen, like a suddenly arrived, mysterious arrow, in splendid isolation on the table's edge.

Meissonier was always careful to keep his props in period. Harnett is not so careful. He gives his monk quill pens to use, the huge books proclaim their antiquity, and the visible pages are clearly the work of medieval scribes; but the book behind the inkwell looks suspiciously like a Tauchnitz Edition paperback and the candlestick is propped on what appears to be a folded newspaper. The vintage of the chair and the frame at the upper right can only be guessed; they do not appear to belong to the era of quill pens.

34

35   William M. Harnett, *The Egyptian Vase*, 1881. Oil on canvas, $3^3/_4 \times 2^3/_4$.
Collection Mr. and Mrs. Donald S. Stralem, New York.

Harnett went to Munich in 1881 and remained there until early 1885. All his Munich pictures bear the name *München* on a line between the signature and the date. He began his career in Munich by reducing the scale of his pictures even below that of his London miniatures of the previous year. Paradoxically, perhaps, along with the new miniaturism goes the highest degree of painterly freedom Harnett ever showed; in this he obviously reflects the popular Munich style of the time. *The Egyptian Vase* is Harnett's smallest known painting. It is so *very* small that he first signed it only on its back, but then he found enough free space at the bottom left to take a signature, if rather oddly, in vertical position.

36   William M. Harnett, *Still Life with Munich Newspaper, Fruit, and Decanter*, 1881.
Oil on canvas, $8^1/_2 \times 7^1/_4$.
University of Massachusetts Art Gallery, Amherst, Massachusetts.

This is the earliest known Harnett to display a compositional formula that he favored above all others in his last years. The objects are arranged pyramidally on a tabletop, moving upward and backward from the table's edge. This upward and backward movement is counterthrusted by the forward and downward movement of a newspaper or a sheet of music (sometimes both) hanging over the edge, while the table edge itself acts as a horizontal stabilizer for the whole performance. This formula appears over and over again in the still lifes of Abraham van Beyeren, Willem Kalf, and other Dutch still-life painters of the seventeenth century. Harnett never practiced it until he went to Europe, but, as we have seen, he favored it strongly after his return. He obviously learned it in the European galleries.

35

36

37 William M. Harnett, *The Old Munich Model*, 1882. Oil on panel, 17 × 14.
Collection Mr. and Mrs. John. L. Gardner, Hamilton, Massachusetts.

> This is Harnett's only known painted portrait,
> although three portrait drawings by him are
> known to exist.

38 William M. Harnett, *Lobster and Pester Lloyd*, 1882. Oil on canvas, $13^1/_2 \times 16^1/_2$.
Collection Dr. and Mrs. Irving Levitt, Southfield, Michigan.

> In 1881 and 1882 Harnett painted at least five still lifes representing the same bright red lobster, with different newspapers over the table's edge and different edibles on top. Whether or not he copied one painted lobster from another, or kept the same real lobster (or its shell) in his studio all those months remains to be discovered.

37

38

39 William M. Harnett, *Deutsche Presse*, 1882. Oil on canvas, $7^1/_2 \times 6$.
Collection Mrs. John Barnes, New York.

Another early example of the compositional formula described in the note to catalogue #36, plus an even greater Munichism in the handling. The framed picture on the wall at the upper right even approaches impressionism. This work represents Harnett's farthest north so far as painterly freedom is concerned.

39

40 William M. Harnett, *Munich Still Life*, 1882. Oil on canvas, $24^5/_8 \times 30^1/_4$.
Dallas Museum of Fine Arts.

Harnett here returns to his older style—crisp, precise, hard of edge, totally un-painterly—but retains the old Dutch compositional convention described under #36 of the present catalogue.

41 William M. Harnett, *Still Life*, 1883. Oil on panel, $8^1/_4 \times 10^3/_4$.
Collection Paul Zuckerman, Franklin, Michigan.

42 William M. Harnett, *Sporting Still Life*, 1883. Oil on panel, $8^1/_4 \times 10^3/_4$.
Collection Paul Zuckerman, Franklin, Michigan.

These two pictures seem to have been intended as a pair. They are identical in size, and while both retain Harnett's devotion to the deep niche at the right, they are balanced compositionally in certain other respects. The main axis in catalogue #41 is in the tankard to the left of center; the main axis in catalogue #42 is in the similar vessel at the right. The tables are draped at opposite ends, and the rightward movement of the pearl-handled knife and the tilted ginger jar in #41 is answered by the powerful leftward thrust of the champagne bottle in #42. Harnett delights in pipes and cigars, but #42 is the only known painting by him to represent cigarettes, which in his time were on the racy, sinful side.

40

41

42

43   William M. Harnett, *After the Hunt* (first version), 1883. Oil on canvas, $52 \times 33^1/_2$.
Private Collection, New York.

44   William M. Harnett, *After the Hunt* (second version), 1883. Oil on canvas, $52^1/_2 \times 36$.
Gallery of Fine Arts, Columbus, Ohio. (Not in exhibition.)

45   William M. Harnett, *After the Hunt* (third version), 1884. Oil on canvas, 55×40.
The Butler Institute of American Art, Youngstown, Ohio.

46   William M. Harnett, *After the Hunt* (fourth version), 1885. Oil on canvas, $70^1/_2 \times 47^1/_2$.
California Palace of the Legion of Honor, San Francisco.

47   William M. Harnett, *Trophy of the Hunt*, 1885. Oil on canvas, $42^1/_2 \times 22$.
Museum of Art, Carnegie Institute, Pittsburgh, Pennsylvania.

48   Adolphe Braun, *After the Hunt*, (ca. 1860). Photograph.

It has long been known that Harnett produced four versions of *After the Hunt*, but the first one to be painted was the last to be found—it came to light only in 1968—and this is the first time that all four have been published together. Regrettably, the four cannot be exhibited together because the second version is pledged to the 1970 centennial of the Metropolitan Museum of Art in New York. (The Metropolitan, for its part, has lent most generously to the present show.)

The still life of hunter's equipment and game is as old as still life itself. Harnett's versions of it are strongly indebted to a series of very large photographs taken about 1860 by the famous Alsatian photographer Adolphe Braun; seven of these survive and one is reproduced herewith. (Braun was one of the first to make a business of making and selling photographs of celebrated paintings and sculptures. He had a large clientele among artists all over Europe, and it is easy to see how Harnett became acquainted with his work.)

The four versions of *After the Hunt* fall into two pairs, not a quartet. The first and second versions (catalogue #43 and #44) are nearly identical in composition, with the gun as a long diagonal axis around which the other objects swing. The principal difference between the first and second versions is in the large dead duck at the lower right; in the first version it is in the dorsal position, in the second in the ventral. The keyhole plates in the two pictures are different in design, the Tyrolean hats are differently punched, and there are very slight differences in the hinges and the winding of the cord around the horn. For the rest, one picture is almost a replica of the other.

The last two versions of *After the Hunt* likewise belong together and are very different from the first two. Antlers, an alpinestock, and a large rabbit have been introduced, and the keyhole plate has taken on the form of a medieval pikeman (a different pikeman each time). The hinges are much longer and more elaborate in the last two versions than in the first two, and in the fourth and largest version some new motifs have been added: the key, the pistol, the horseshoe, and the canteen. But the introduction of new subject matter is far

43

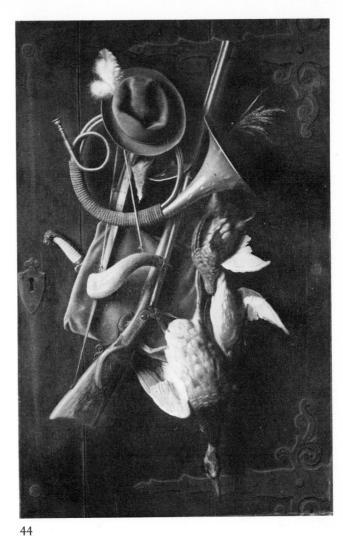

44

less important than the new compositional devices that are employed; these reach their climax in the fourth version.

Version four rests, compositionally speaking, upon a great X form; its upper arms are the antlers, its lower arms the gunstock and the sword hilt. (The sword, which lies to the left and plays no structural role in the three other paintings, has now been brought around to the right.) Over the great X just described, the horn, the hat, and the horseshoe describe a series of circular shapes, diminishing in size and conveying a sense of upward movement. This upward movement is counterthrusted by the downward pull of the game birds, the rabbit, and the canteen. The alpinestock (which levitates, totally unsupported and unattached) reinforces the diagonal of the gun barrel, which is in danger of losing its powerful thrust because of the new objects introduced into the composition.

The fourth version of *After the Hunt* was painted in Paris in 1885 and exhibited at the spring Salon of that year. Harnett, as he later told a newspaper interviewer, went to Paris because he was fed up with the constant criticism of his work in Munich. Munich liked a dashing, brushy, painterly style, and Harnett's immaculate realism, with all brushwork carefully concealed, seemed old-fashioned to the teachers and critics there. A review of his work in a Munich paper speaks, however, of a hit he had made with the general public in 1883 with a picture of a rabbit, obviously much like *Trophy of*

45

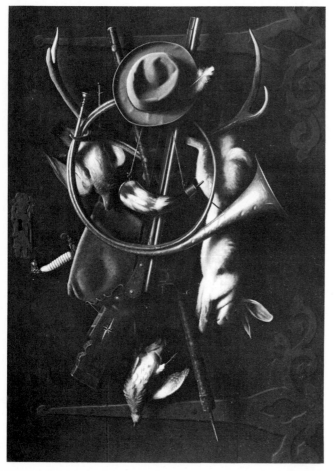

46

the Hunt; this rabbit, in complete and minute detail, is taken over by the last two versions of *After the Hunt*. In other words, the artist had good reason to think the rabbit would please, and, playing the game for blood against official Munich taste, he uses that rabbit in the last two variations of his big hunting picture.

Harnett brought the fourth version of *After the Hunt* with him when he returned from Paris in 1886 and sold it to Theodore Stewart, who hung it in his celebrated saloon at 8 Warren Street, New York, a step from City Hall. There it was such a success that making adaptations and paraphrases of it for bars and hotels became a major industry among American artists for decades. Jefferson David Chalfant plagiarized it shamelessly. Alexander Pope, Richard LaBarre Goodwin, William Keane, and Charles Meurer painted versions of it which are in the present exhibition. Many more such versions could have been added.

47

48

49 William M. Harnett, *Still Life with Tankard*, 1885. Oil on panel, $16^{1}/_{2} \times 20$.
Collection Mr. and Mrs. Mortimer Spiller, Buffalo, New York.

On the back of the panel is an old inscription in an unknown hand: "Painted by W. M. Harnett of Paris." This is probably the latest of Harnett's European pictures extant. It sums up what he learned abroad: the compositional formulas of the old Dutch masters (see the notes to #36 in the present catalogue), a certain miniaturism (all the objects are represented smaller than the scale of life), and considerable elegance in subject matter. This last trait we have not had occasion to point out earlier in this catalogue, but it is very important. The nineteenth century judged still life almost entirely on the basis of its subject matter, and it delighted in the representation of rich, rare, and curious things. The copper tankard, the Roman lamp, the jewel chest behind it, the vellum-bound book, and the sheet of Gregorian neumes from a missal were (or were supposed to be) antiques of great price, but Harnett's own vernacularistic bent asserts itself in the worn velvet drape on the table.

50 William M. Harnett. *Golden Horseshoe*, 1886. Oil on canvas, $15^{1}/_{2} \times 13^{1}/_{2}$.
Collection Mr. and Mrs. James W. Alsdorf, Winnetka, Illinois.

Harnett's vernacularistic bent reasserts itself with a vengeance here, immediately on his return from Europe.

49

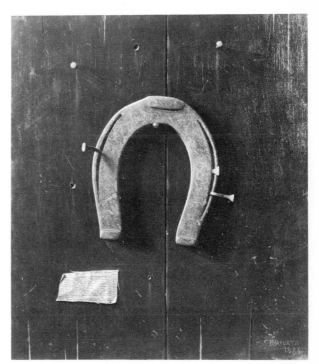

50

51 William M. Harnett, *Mr. Hulings' Rack Picture*, 1888. Oil on canvas, 30 × 25.
Courtesy of Kennedy Galleries, Inc., New York.

This painting, one of two rack pictures by Harnett known to exist, came to light in the spring of 1969 after many years in the dark of junk shops and secondhand stores in the Philadelphia area. It was painted for George Hulings, a Philadelphia dry-goods merchant and friend of Harnett. It contains four calling cards, two government postcards, a Western Union telegram, eight envelopes, and a folded piece of paper inscribed "...ary Commandery No. 36," with a cross between the "No." and the "36."

Two of the envelopes—the yellow and blue ones at the left of the rack, over the Western Union telegram—turn their backs to the spectator, so that no address can be read on them; these envelopes, furthermore, have not been opened. All the other envelopes *have* been opened, and they are addressed to Hulings either at his store, 1300 South Fourth Street, or his home, 406 Wharton Street. With one exception, the envelopes addressed to Hulings also reveal the names and addresses of their senders; this is the only rack picture the writer has ever seen that reveals this characteristic.

The calling cards were from the following:

S. W. Creadick, physician, 1314 South...
H. A. Rowan, "supt.," 322 Reed Street
George W. Isard, clerk, no address

Hulings' correspondents, their addresses, and their professions, as disclosed by Gopsill's Philadelphia City Directory for 1887, are as follows:

William McCarter, painter,
  256–258 South Fifth Street
William McPherson, M.D., druggist,
  347 Wharton Street

J. Wesley Bowen, undertaker,
  1026 South Second Street
C. W. Bickley, minister, 1236 South Fourth Street

Creadick's street address is covered by the tape at the top left of the rack, but the card there provides his office hours. The addresses given indicate that all these men were Hulings' neighbors. The meaning of the mysterious piece of folded paper at the bottom right is clarified by Hulings' obituary in the Philadelphia *Public Ledger* of January 9, 1902. This notice states that Hulings was a thirty-second-degree Mason and also "a member of the Milita Lodge, No. 295, of St. Mary Commandery, and of the Consistory."

On June 11, 1895, the Philadelphia *Item* published a story in which, among other things, it asserted that Hulings possessed a painting by Harnett which represented a card rack made of tape containing a number of cards and letters from Hulings' friends. The reference is clearly to the picture now under consideration. This picture was not known to exist, however, until last year. Many years earlier a copy of the *Item* story fell into unscrupulous hands, and on May 24, 1940, The Museum of Modern Art in New York acquired a rack picture by John Frederick Peto with a faked Harnett signature and a faked inscription on one of its envelopes addressed to Mr. Hulings of Wharton Street. This painting attained great prominence as a Harnett until the present writer demonstrated that it is a Peto. It is in the current exhibition under its proper attribution, and further information about the forgery involved will be found in the notes discussing it.

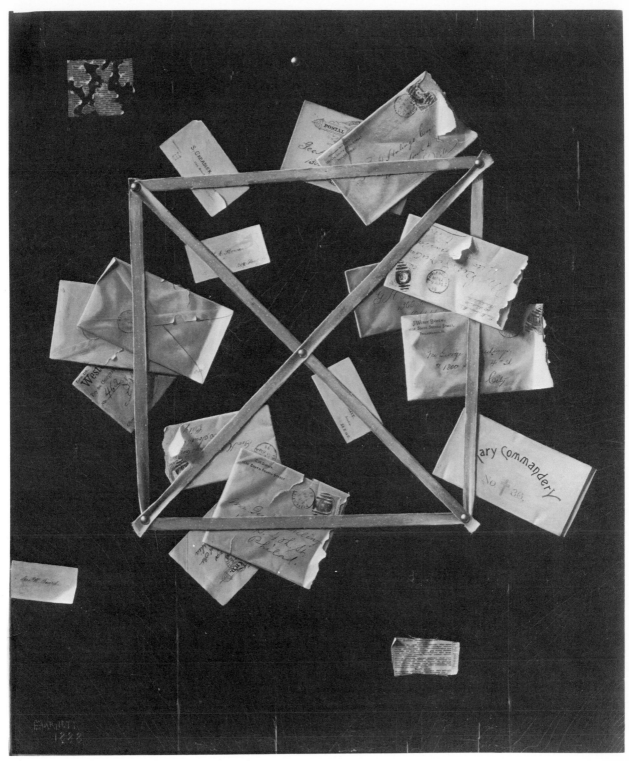

51

52   William M. Harnett, *Music and Good Luck*, 1888. Oil on canvas, 40 × 30.
Lent by The Metropolitan Museum of Art, Catherine Lorillard Wolfe Fund, 1963.

The violin has been a highly favored still-life subject ever since still life first existed, partly because it occupies little depth, partly because its baroque curves are beautiful, and partly because it evokes pleasant associations. Harnett painted the instrument often, and a chromolithograph after his painting of 1886, *The Old Violin*, spawned even more imitations than *After the Hunt*.

No one knew better than Harnett how shadows can be used to create relief, and this is his finest shadow picture. The partly opened cabinet door is an old Dutch motif with which he probably became acquainted in Europe.

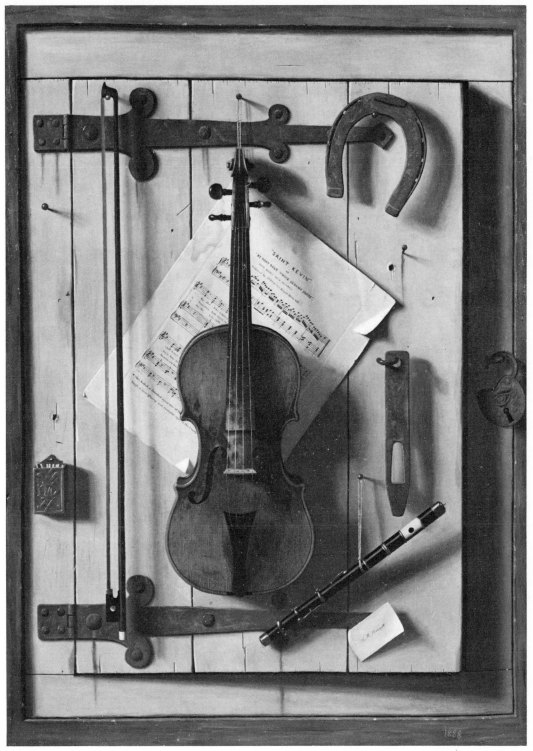

52

53   William M. Harnett, *Still Life*, 1888. Oil on canvas, 14 × 17.
     Lent by The Metropolitan Museum of Art, Bequest of Susan Vanderpoel Clark, 1967.

The Dutch jar—one specific Dutch jar—is the most characteristic of Harnett's models during the last years of his life. He displays it from every angle, and the student of his work becomes quite as familiar with the cow and the windmill on its other side as with the houses, fence, and trees that appear in the present painting. Jars like this one are very common in seventeenth-century Dutch still life, and Harnett obviously uses it in tribute to his celebrated predecessors. The flute solo, *Hélas, quelle douleur*, is also a favorite Harnett model.

54   William M. Harnett, *The Faithful Colt*, 1890. Oil on canvas, 22¹/₂ × 18¹/₂.
     Wadsworth Atheneum, Hartford, Connecticut: The Ella Gallup Sumner and Mary Catlin Sumner Collection.

The Faithful Colt was the pilot picture of the Harnett revival and hence of the revival of American *trompe l'œil* in general. It was brought to Edith Gregor Halpert, director of the Downtown Gallery in New York, in 1935. Mrs. Halpert had never heard of Harnett nor had anyone else in the New York art world at that time. Mrs. Halpert realized, as she later told the writer of these lines, that a man who painted that well didn't paint only one picture. She started to investigate, and...

53

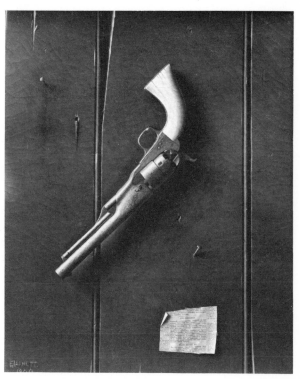

54

55 William M. Harnett, *The Old Cupboard Door*, 1889. Oil on canvas, 61$^1/_2$ × 41. Graves Art Gallery, Sheffield, England.

This is the only Harnett known to exist in any collection, public or private, in Europe. Rather oddly, it is not one of the numerous pictures which Harnett painted and sold there. It was painted to order for William B. Bement, one of the great Victorian collectors of Philadelphia. Immediately after Bement's death in 1899, the picture was bought by H. H. Andrew of Sheffield, who forthwith deposited it in the Mappin Art Gallery, now the Graves Art Gallery, in that city, and there it has remained. This will be its first public showing in the United States.

The picture is a veritable anthology of *trompe l'œil* effects—the door stopping the eye at the picture plane, the flat objects (music, hinges, violin, key), the small objects on a shallowly protruding ledge. For *trompe l'œil* painters to represent objects under glass is common enough, but for the transparent material to be the oiled head of a tambourine is something else again.

This painting, by the way, is Harnett's only known work for the year 1889. He spent most of that year in hospitals and spas in search of relief for crippling rheumatism. He never regained his health completely and did not return to his old tempo, although the quality of his work never fell off, and his last work—*Old Models*, in the Museum of Fine Arts, Boston—is one of his very finest.

55

The key to Peto is that he was a failure. The early part of his career is dominated by the desire to succeed, and his work clearly reflects that fact. In the latter part of his career he was totally indifferent to success because success was indifferent to *him*; since nobody cared, he might as well do as he pleased, and he pleased to do some very remarkable things.

Peto was born in Philadelphia, was educated at the Pennsylvania Academy of the Fine Arts at the same time as Harnett, and seems to have been on excellent terms with him until Harnett went to Europe in 1880. Peto took over many ideas from Harnett but made them entirely his own; in the use of the card-rack motif, however, Peto seems to have been the forerunner and Harnett the follower. Be all that as it may, the personalities, styles, and careers of the two men were totally different.

From 1879 to 1889, Peto played the professional art game. He maintained studios in Philadelphia, sent pictures regularly to the annual exhibitions at the Pennsylvania Academy of the Fine Arts and elsewhere, did some photography and decorative sculpture, and ran around Philadelphia doing commercial jobs of painting and design. None of it paid off very well, and before long Peto's avocation proved to be better business than his profession.

His avocation was playing the cornet. In those days before electrical amplification, there was a job for a cornet player in leading the mass singing at the camp meetings in Island Heights, New Jersey. Peto started going there around 1887; in 1889 he built a house and moved there for good. He lost touch with the big-city art world, stopped sending to the exhibitions, and before long was totally isolated. The camp meetings moved away, leaving as their legacy in Island Heights a bone-dry law which has lasted to this day. Because Island Heights was dry, it became a favorite summer resort for genteel families with children, and little Mr. Peto, whose wife took in summer boarders, sold little souvenir still lifes to the nice summer people; these are now scattered all over the Eastern seaboard and keep turning up in both likely and unlikely places.

Peto also painted many larger pictures at Island Heights. He doubtless sold some, but he could not have sold many because he left a vast number of canvases unfinished. Over and over again he would start a picture, carry it close to completion, and then abandon it. He would also paint pictures over other pictures; X ray has revealed as many as three paintings on a single piece of canvas. At times he would paint a picture, inscribe its title and date on its back, and then, later, paint another picture on top of the first one without changing the original inscription. Peto's work as a whole is therefore a wild, disorderly heap in which only the general outlines of chronological progression can be made out; and it is full of pitfalls and surprises of many kinds.

Around 1905, not long before Peto died, an unscrupulous Philadephia dealer carted away a consignment of his pictures and never accounted for them. Soon Petos with faked Harnett signatures began to appear on the Philadelphia market, and they reappeared thirty years later when the modern revival of Harnett and his school was started. Consequently, confused and inaccurate criteria for Harnett's style were implanted in the art world at the outset of the modern revival. Establishing correct criteria required a bit of a battle, but ultimately they *were* established, and in the process Peto, Haberle, Goodwin, Chalfant, Pope, Dubreuil—indeed, the entire school of American *trompe l'œil* still life after 1870—was brought to light.

It is difficult for the modern sensibility to understand the reasons for Peto's failure in his own time. It was mainly the result of his vernacularism, his delight in commonplace objects. The nineteenth century placed a far greater emphasis on subject matter than we do. A still life was good if it represented pleasant things, bad if it didn't. Harnett learned this lesson early. Peto never learned it. He defied it, and so he was ignored. But his "ugly" subject matter is a major source of his appeal to the present day.

A strongly tragic feeling infuses much of Peto's still life. He understood the pathos of the object as did very few artists in his time, and it is not too much to draw a parallel between his fascination with the tattered, torn, discarded, burned, and violated, and the similar fascination displayed by such artists as Kurt Schwitters and Robert Rauschenberg. Peto demonstrates, as does no other painter in history, the fact that still life can be a tragic art. In the tragic tone of his work, in his dark palette, and in his personal isolation, he presents striking parallels to other major American painters of his era, notably Thomas Eakins, Albert Ryder, and the later Winslow Homer. Peto, alone among American still-life painters of his time, is in the main stream.

56 John Frederick Peto, *Old Souvenirs*, 1881. Oil on canvas, 27 × 22.
Lent by The Metropolitan Museum of Art, Bequest of Oliver Burr Jennings, 1968.

Peto is peculiarly the master of the rack picture. Harnett is known to have painted only two such works and probably did no more, but Peto painted dozens of them. During the first period of his career (Philadelphia, 1879–1889), they were produced largely as ornaments for places of business, and Peto called them "office boards." This work is probably an office board that didn't sell and that Peto therefore patched up to remove its business references after the prospective patron to whom it was shown declined it.

The newspaper is dated 1881; and this is probably the date when the work was originally completed, but the upside-down postcard at the right seems to be addressed to Peto at 1027 Chestnut Street, where he maintained a studio only in 1887. Peto's office boards commonly contained portraits of the business or professional men for whom they were made, and these were invariably in the form of *trompe l'œil* painted photographs. The photograph here is a portrait of Peto's daughter, but X ray reveals that it was painted over another portrait in similar style. Peto was not married until 1887, and his daughter was born in 1893, so her face could not have been added until 1900 or thereabouts. The large, frayed, paper-bound book hanging over the insurance company's calendar is also, quite legibly, a later addition intended to conceal all but the upper, decorative corners of that advertisement. Unraveling such palimpsests is typical of the problems that beset one in trying to make sense out of Peto's work. Add a faked Harnett signature, like the one at the bottom here, and the madness of the situation is beautifully complete.

The rack proper is typical of those Peto designed early in his career; it is really four racks in one and involves a great number of tapes. Later racks were to be much simpler in pattern. The general style of the picture is rather loose and stringy, and the radiant, soft, powdery texture which is the sign manual of Peto in his great days is not to be observed at all.

Great still-life painters employ only a limited repertoire of models. One can conceive of a still-life painter's using an entirely different set of models for each painting, but that is not the way the great men of the tradition think and work. Peto has a predilection for the commonest things in his environment, and he uses them over and over again. That little green pamphlet entitled "Report" recurs many times, each time with its date changed to coincide with the date of the painting. The little tan-orange envelope inscribed "Important Information Inside" proclaims its little mystery in many Petos, and the "dinner check" is an old friend. These were all just little scraps of paper or cardboard, but John Frederick Peto cherished them for years and wove them into his still-life compositions innumerable times. They were also clearly defined rectangular shapes.

56

57   John Frederick Peto, *Abandoned Treasures*, (1884). Oil on canvas, 20×24.
     Private Collection, New York.

The loose, easy style of Peto's Philadelphia period is again observable here and, like the preceding picture, this canvas is a palimpsest. The ridges of pigment created by a grid pattern painted on the canvas underneath the box of books are clearly visible. This grid pattern resembles that of the windows in Peto's house at Island Heights. The Harnett signature at the lower right is, of course, a forgery.

58   John Frederick Peto, *Old Friends*, (ca. 1887). Oil on academy board, $8^3/_4 \times 11^1/_2$.
     Private Collection, New York.

The style of Peto's maturity asserts itself here: soft in edge, radiant and powdery in texture, powerful in contrasts of light and shade. The complete absence of differentiated textures among the objects represented would belie the faked Harnett signature at the lower right if that signature could not be proved a forgery by other means; but a considerable chain of other circumstances, including the fact that the iron lard lamp remains to this day in Peto's studio, convicts it beyond question.

57

58

59 John Frederick Peto, *Lincoln and the Pfleger Stretcher*, 1898. Oil on canvas, 10 × 14.
New Britain Museum of American Art, New Britain, Connecticut.

This painting is one of seven Petos known to the present writer which bear on their backs the title *The Old Mill*; this one is also dated, 1898. One or two of these canvases actually contain pictures of an old mill; the others probably did so at one time but were painted over.

Lincoln and the Pfleger Stretcher is Peto's genuflection to the Zeuxis-Parrhasios legend and is identical with William M. Davis's version of that legend, #17 in the present catalogue. No one knows if Davis got the idea from Peto, Peto from Davis, or both from a common source; perhaps they invented it independently.

The Pfleger Patent was a type of stretcher which Peto used throughout much of his career.

Its very distinctive form, beveled and beaded, was a factor in establishing the differential diagnosis between his work and Harnett's at a time when they were confused with each other in the minds of the art world. The oval Lincoln portrait is taken from a very popular engraving by J. C. Buttre after a photograph by Mathew Brady; like the torn-off labels and metal number-plates which appear throughout his work, Peto repeats it to an obsessive degree. The Lincoln portrait in this painting is unfinished, and in a very vital area, around the mouth. Only a few more strokes would have completed the painting. This failure to finish a work when it was all *but* finished is characteristic of Peto in his later years.

60 John Frederick Peto, *Job Lot, Cheap*, n.d. Oil on canvas, 38³/₄ × 29¹/₄.
Private Collection, New York.

Peto sometimes took ideas from Harnett, as he clearly did in this case. The Harnett version (#27 in the present catalogue) was painted in 1878. The Peto, undated, belongs stylistically with the richest period of the artist's career and is therefore at least twenty years younger than the Harnett. One does not need to expatiate any longer on the radiant textures and powerful contrasts of light and shade which are so characteristic of Peto. Here he sets Harnett's books in an architectural setting worthy of Josef Albers or any other geometric-abstract painter of recent years, and gives the whole the tragic tone which is uniquely his.

59

60

61 John Frederick Peto, *Still Life*, n.d. Oil on academy board, 9 × 6.
Collection Mr. and Mrs. Alfred Frankenstein, San Francisco.

Typical of Peto's little summer-boarder pictures and also typical of one of his subtle compositional devices. The spectator's eye is placed on a level with the edge of the table, so that one sees nothing of its retreating surface; to a naïve observer, the horizontal strip at the bottom of the painting has no depth at all. This enables Peto to place the objects at the picture plane, in the best *trompe l'œil* style, yet makes it possible for one to read them as standing back from the edge if one is minded so to do. But for all its *trompe l'œil* arrangement, the "skin" of the painting is brushy, rough, and far from imitative of natural appearances.

62 John Frederick Peto, *Hanging Carpet Bag, Hat, and Umbrella*, (ca. 1890). Oil on canvas, 20 × 12.
Collection Mr. and Mrs. Mortimer Spiller, Buffalo, New York.

There is a strong bucolic streak in Peto, which is one of the things that sets his personality apart from that of the intensely urban Harnett. Harnett never painted a landscape in his life. Peto often did, and he sometimes uses still-life objects typical of rural ways. Two of his favorite rural objects are the umbrella and the farmer's hat used in this and the immediately subsequent painting.

63 John Frederick Peto, *Market Basket, Hat, and Umbrella*, (after 1890). Oil on canvas, 12 × 18.
Layton Art Gallery Collection, Milwaukee Art Center, Milwaukee, Wisconsin.

Another variation on the bucolic theme. The umbrella is unfinished to the left of the handle of the basket, yet its very unfinishedness helps to set off the hat most dramatically and makes for a more effective painting than if it had been completed.

61

62

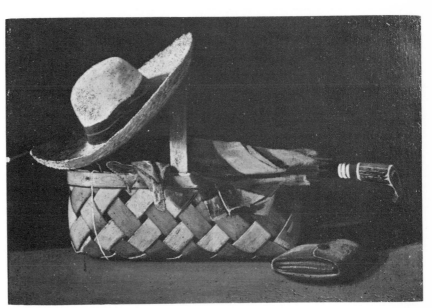

63

64 John Frederick Peto, *Old Companions*, 1904. Oil on canvas, 22 × 31.
Collection Mr. and Mrs. J. William Middendorf II, New York.

Peto's house in Island Heights is full of shelves set high, often in impractical places. He simply liked to have objects on shelves around him. This and the next two paintings all use the same shelf, each time seen in the same way as the table in catalogue #61; in other words, the spectator's eye is placed on a level with the edge of the shelf, its retreating surface is not seen (except for an ambiguous moment at the extreme left in catalogue #65), and depth is thereby eliminated. The relationship of the objects to the edge of the shelf is not explicitly stated and, except for those objects which protrude over the edge, can be read in several ways.

In each painting the shelf is piled high with dilapidated, worn-out, discarded things. This symphony of rags and tatters reaches its climax, perhaps, in the great, open, darkly hollow lantern of catalogue #66.

The book hanging over the edge in catalogue #64 is unfinished, but the picture is the better for it, and that, perhaps, is why it was never completed.

65 John Frederick Peto, *Still Life with Lard Oil Lamp*, n.d. Oil on canvas, 13$^1/_2$ × 23$^1/_2$.
The Newark Museum, Bequest of Dr. Donald M. Dougall, Newark, New Jersey.

66 John Frederick Peto, *Lamps of Other Days*, n.d. Oil on canvas, 27$^1/_8$ × 36$^1/_8$.
Amon Carter Museum of Western Art, Fort Worth, Texas.

64

65

66

67 John Frederick Peto, *Old Time Letter Rack*, 1894. Oil on canvas, $30 \times 25^1/_8$.
The Museum of Modern Art, New York,
Gift of Nelson A. Rockefeller, 1940.

This work was given to The Museum of Modern Art as a Harnett and attained considerable celebrity as such until 1948, when the present writer demonstrated, by means of stylistic and iconographic analysis, that it is actually a Peto. Full details of that analysis may be found in the writer's book, *After the Hunt* (Berkeley and Los Angeles: University of California Press, 1969, second edition). It may be summarized as follows:

(1) The picture is in Peto's style, with his radiant, powdery color and soft edges, his restless movement, and his emphasis upon the ramshackle and discarded.

(2) The postmarks on the letters are dated late in 1894, two years after Harnett's death; one of them is from Lerado, Ohio, where Peto's wife was born and where he is known to have been in the fall of 1894; and the white postcard at the top right was not issued until that year. The inscription on this card, "...lings/...and Wharton St./ Philadelphia/Penn." is a late addition, placed on the canvas with pen and ink, over a pre-existing inscription, now illegible. Finally, in 1948 a buried Peto signature, just to the left of the faked Harnett signature, was discovered by Sheldon Keck under a coat of paint that had been placed there to cover it up.

Nineteen years later, Miss Jean Volkmer, conservationist at The Museum of Modern Art, found that the painting had a superfluous lining canvas on its back. She removed it and uncovered the following inscription on the back of the original canvas:

OLD TIME LETTER RACK
11.94
John F. Peto
Artist
ISLAND HEIGHTS
N.J.

The second line of this inscription is, of course, the date, expressed in Peto's habitual fashion: November, 1894, precisely the date of the Lerado postmark on the blue envelope. The faked inscription, "...lings/...and Wharton St./Philadelphia/Penn." was obviously placed on the canvas in order to make a show of identifying it with Harnett's rack picture for George Hulings (#51 in the present catalogue), which at that time was not known to exist, though a description of it had survived in an old newspaper account.

67

68   John Frederick Peto, *Bowie Knife, Keyed Bugle, and Canteen,* n.d. Oil on canvas, 40 × 30.
Collection Amanda K. Berls, Amagansett, New York.

Objects hanging loosely before a door provide Peto with one of his favorite compositional formulas. This formula is also his clearest tribute to the orthodox *trompe l'œil* tradition: a door or wall at the picture plane with objects protruding from it, but never very far, into the spectator's space. The bowie knife, the powder horn, and the keyed bugle were three of Peto's favorite models. According to family tradition, the artist's father, who served in the Civil War, picked up the bowie knife on the battlefield of Gettysburg.

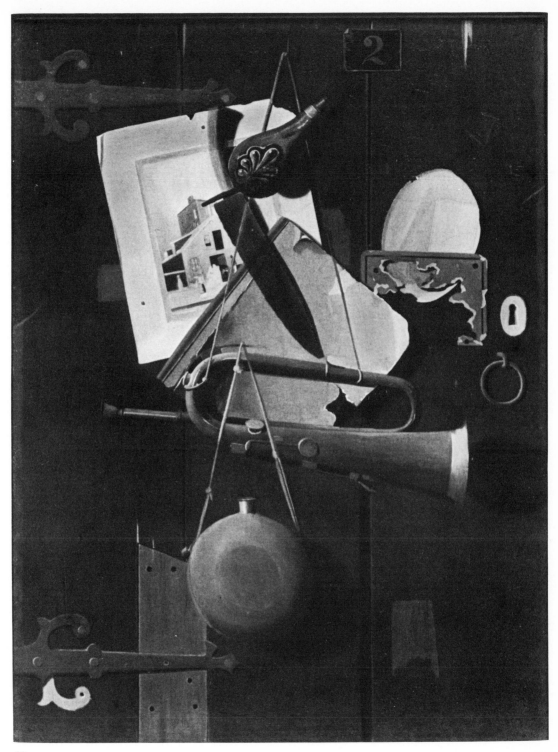

68

69 John Frederick Peto, *Old Reminiscences*, 1900. Oil on canvas, 30 × 25.
The Phillips Collection, Washington, D.C.

Another Peto rack which was once famous as a Harnett because it is "signed" with a fake address to that artist on the letter at the right. The date, 1900, painted as if whittled into the door at the lower left, seems to have bothered no one at the time of the Harnett revival, even though it was known that Harnett had died in 1892; it was interpreted as a little surrealistic *jeu d'esprit* on Harnett's part. This attribution of modern motivations to artists of the nineteenth century, and the concomitant failure to make any effort at discovering what their own motivations may have been, explains why the Harnett forgery problem existed for so long and was so difficult to clear up. It was the result of a deep-lying psychological failure on the part of contemporary critics and historians; the iconographic aspect of the problem—the date or provenance of one object or another—is very minor compared to this. *Old Reminiscences* is, of course, full of characteristic Peto models: the Lincoln portrait, the small green book at the left of the rack, the bookmaker's ticket numbered (in this instance) 905, the dinner check, the "Proprietor" envelope, the card of Dr. S. H. Jones, and so on.

70 John Frederick Peto, *Rack Picture with Dutch Jar*, n.d. Oil on canvas, 40 × 30.
Courtesy of Kennedy Galleries, Inc., New York.

Harnett often ornaments his doors with long, extremely fancy hinges; Peto's adaptation of this motif, characteristically, takes the form of very blunt and simple hinges which have rotted from their moorings. The Dutch jar here is also an adaptation of a favorite Harnett model, but it is greatly simplified in shape and totally devoid of decoration. To draw modern parallels to the work of old artists is not quite the same thing as ascribing modern motivations to them (although it comes perilously close), and one can scarcely refrain from pointing out the modern-abstract feeling of this Peto jar. It is an Ozenfant at the very least; maybe it is even a Morandi.

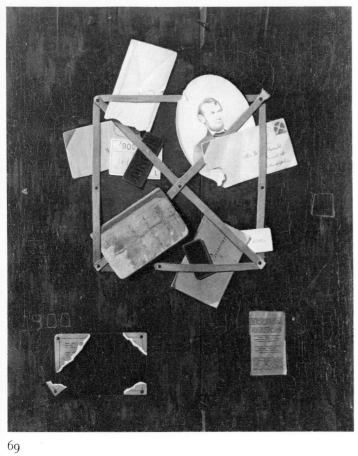

69

70

71 John Frederick Peto, *Still Life with Candle and Books*, n.d. Oil on canvas, $30 \times 22^1/_4$.
Hirschl and Adler Galleries, Inc., New York.

Peto's modeling of objects in light assumes an extreme and very personal form here: the light flooding the objects on one side and throwing the other side into very deep darkness, sometimes with a bright, long highlight dividing the one area from the other, as in the candlestick of the present picture. The precise vertical division of the ink bottle into light and dark halves has a curiously cubist look.

71

JOHN HABERLE
1858–1933

Peto is moved by the pathos of used-up things. Haberle is wry and wacky, full of bravado, self-congratulating virtuosity, and sly flamboyance. He works largely within an old tradition, that of the *trompe l'œil* still life in painted line, with a minimum of modeling and no exploitation of color and tone except for purposes of strictly local description. This tradition is usually observed in watercolor; it lends itself well to comedy, and sometimes shades off into an expression scarcely distinguishable from the humorous cartoon. It is poles away from Harnett's sumptuosity, careful balances, and well-modeled volumes, and is equally far from Peto's sensitivity in matters of tone and hue. Haberle, to be sure, paints no watercolors, and his comedy is far subtler than that of the newspaper cartoon. He has a strong vernacular streak in his makeup and was a pop artist seventy years before Roy Lichtenstein was ever heard of.

Haberle lived all his life in New Haven and worked for many years as a preparator of exhibits in the paleontological museum of Yale University. He is also said to have done illustrations for Yale scientific publications, but if so, he received no public credit for this work. His great career lasted only from 1887 to about 1898; he began to have trouble with his eyes; henceforth he painted seldom and then mostly in the loose, impressionistic manner suggested by *A Dishpan of Flowers*, catalogue #81 below. But in 1909 he came forth with the recently discovered *Night*, probably the greatest *trompe l'œil* painting ever produced in America. It is being shown a national audience for the first time in the present exhibition.

72   John Haberle, *The Changes of Time*, 1888. Oil on canvas, $23^3/_4 \times 15^3/_4$.
Collection Mr. and Mrs. Marvin Preston, Ferndale, Michigan.

To a light gray door are pasted many types of American currency, from a Connecticut Colony twenty-shilling note of 1773 through various types of Federal greenbacks and Confederate notes down to a five-dollar bill of the series of 1886. There is a similar progression of coins and postage stamps, including one from Canada, and some of the stamps are pasted across the bottom crack of the door. There is also a hair-raisingly problematical key escutcheon in the form of a grinning brass satyr head which is firmly nailed across the crack at the left. Balancing the key escutcheon, at the right, are two brass hinges, one in the form of a butterfly and the other in the form of two scrolls, back to back. Toward the top of the door a cracked magnifying glass with a worn black handle rests on a carefully edited notice of the painting with which Haberle had made his debut in the annual exhibitions at the National Academy of Design the previous year: "entirely with the brush and with the naked eye/*Imitation*, no 362, by J. Haberle…a/.emarkable piece of imitation of natural ob-/jects and a most deceptive *trompe l'oil*" [sic]. The newspaper clippings in Haberle's paintings, unlike those in the paintings of Harnett and Peto, are always legible and are always in praise of Haberle. The one just quoted is a pastiche of at least two separate reviews. The main thing omitted is the observation, by the art critic of the New York *Evening Post*, that *Imitation*, "…*without being in any sense a work of art*, is a remarkable piece of imitation," etc. The newspaper reviewers of that time always wrote about Harnett, Peto, and Haberle in that way.

To go back to *The Changes of Time*, the door has its own frame, and on it, at the upper left, is a "cigarette picture" of a woman covering part of the date, 1888, which has been painted as if incised

in the wood. At the bottom, in the crack between the door and its frame, a small piece of paper protrudes, indicating that the door is that of a cabinet, crammed full of something—probably money—made totally unattainable by that satyr-headed key plate nailed across the crack at the left.

The frame around the entire picture is painted and is an integral part of the canvas. The faces of all the Presidents from Washington to Benjamin Harrison, identified by their names and dates of administration, appear on it as if carved in wooden medallions, but in a very curious order. Washington is in the center at the top, flanked by Jefferson and Adams. The subsequent Presidents alternate, left and right across the top bar of the frame and criss-cross from one side bar to the other, until we get to Hayes, when they proceed in direct succession to Benjamin Harrison, who had just entered on his term of office at the time the picture was completed. There is a small coin over the lower part of the Harrison medallion. It has

slipped from the place where it was originally tacked, just below and to the right of the cluster of six stamps on the lower part of the door, and there it has left a ghost image of itself.

The four medallions at the lower right corner are empty. They are partly covered by a violet-colored envelope addressed to Haberle in New Haven and postmarked New York with the date, "'88." On top of this is a tintype self-portrait. The small corner of the letter which protrudes from the envelope is one of Haberle's most delicious feats of virtuosity; one can almost hear him chuckle with delighted self-approval as one studies it. No complete words are legible, but it is nonetheless apparent that the more boldly stroked letters are in mirror writing, while the interlined fainter letters are not. In other words, the paper is quite thin, the mirror writing is on the reverse side of the first sheet, and the fainter letters are on the obverse side of a sheet beneath. "Entirely with the brush and with the naked eye."!

73 John Haberle, *Fresh Roasted*, 1887. Oil on canvas, $11 \times 22^1/_4$.
Collection Wilbur C. Munnecke, Leland, Michigan.

One of the oldest tricks in the *trompe l'œil* game is the painting of flat objects under broken glass. Usually this trick leads to pictures of engravings, stamps, and similar flat papers which have been framed but the glass of which has been shattered. Haberle's American vernacularism leads him to

use the same device for peanuts in a bin with a broken-glass cover through which a measuring can protrudes; but the peanuts inevitably crowd forward toward the picture plane and one of them has fallen through the broken glass to be caught by the edge of the frame.

74 John Haberle, *A Favorite*, (ca. 1890). Oil on canvas, $14^1/_2 \times 11^1/_2$.
Museum of Fine Arts, Springfield, Massachusetts.

Into a flat board, held with screws at each corner except the upper right (where the screw has fallen out), a long, rectangular hole has been cut. A cigar-box lid has been inserted into this hole and is held there, most precariously, by a single toothpick inserted into it and into the edge of the larger board at the right of the hole. A little door has been

cut into the cigar-box lid; it is held at the top with a leather hinge and is to be pulled up with a loop of string. If one did pull it up, one would see nothing at all; one would come face to face with the Abyss. The rest of the painting needs no description.

73

74

75 John Haberle, *Slate*, (ca. 1895). Oil on canvas, 11 × 9.
Collection Mr. and Mrs. Ferdinand H. Davis, New York.

Haberle was fond of painting slates with messages, no longer meaningful, chalked on them and with the chalk hanging by a string in front. They provide the perfect, textbook definition of the *trompe l'œil* style.

Haberle often signs his work with a self-portrait in the form of a tintype or with a little self-caricature like the one in the present painting, which shows him as a dancing brave with a feather in his hair and with his name beneath broken into syllables in a feeble effort to make it look "Indian." These childish, scrawly little self-caricatures of Haberle's look astonishingly like the children's drawings which appear occasionally on the walls in seventeenth-century Dutch still lifes. Whether in Amsterdam, circa 1600, or New Haven, circa 1900, the five-year-old style remains the same.

76 John Haberle, *Torn in Transit*, n.d. Oil on canvas, 13 × 17.
Collection Amanda K. Berls, Amagansett, New York.

As is pointed out in the introduction to this catalogue, a *trompe l'œil* landscape is unthinkable, if only because it would have to be as big as its own subject. The landscape here is not intended to be seen as a landscape; it is intended to be seen as a *painting* of a landscape, and that is something quite different. In other words, the painting inside the torn paper is a still-life object; the paper, the labels on it, and the string and its shadows are of proper scale and flatness for *trompe l'œil*, and are so handled.

The painted landscape as still-life object is one of Haberle's best inventions. He rings many changes on it; one of the best is catalogue #78 below. It is not surprising that with ideas like this, the *trompe l'œil* tradition really comes to its end, for when you have reached the stage at which the whole point of *trompe l'œil* painting is that three-fourths of it is NOT *trompe l'œil*, there is nowhere else to go.

75

76

77   John Haberle, *Can You Break a Five?*, (ca. 1885). Oil on canvas, $7^1/_2 \times 11^1/_2$.
Collection Dr. and Mrs. Irving Levitt, Southfield, Michigan.

Stories of arrests for counterfeiting because of the painting of paper money are the Van Gogh's ear of the American *trompe l'œil* saga. There are official records to show that Harnett was warned by the authorities to cease and desist from painting or exhibiting such things, and Haberle may have been in trouble over them, too. At all events, in this painting, as in at least one other, he carefully and defiantly sets down the warning against counterfeiting that was then published on American currency. (It is on the fragment of the dollar bill beneath the five.) Whatever truth there may be in these stories about painters being punished as counterfeiters, they have been greatly exaggerated in the popular literature; they are really another version of Zeuxis and Parrhasios.

It was typical of Haberle's temperament to paint paper money because he knew it was against the law; but the real reason why Haberle and all the rest of them painted currency is that it is flat. As usual, the newspaper clipping is from a review in praise of Haberle.

78   John Haberle, *Clock*, n.d. Oil on canvas, $26 \times 15^1/_2$.
Hirschl and Adler Galleries, Inc., New York.

Another example, much subtler than *Torn in Transit*, of *trompe l'œil* painting *per se* combined with landscape painting in a commonplace, far from *trompe l'œil* style but presented as a *trompe l'œil* object. The realistic effect of this counterfeit clock is enhanced by its being tacked to a boxlike stretcher which is about as deep as a real clock of that height would be.

This picture stood for years in the half-dark of a high shelf in a stairwell in Haberle's house in New Haven, and the writer of these lines passed it many times before he realized that it was a picture and not a clock.

Many years after Haberle, Frank Stella was to use deep stretchers on his abstract paintings in order to underline their thingness, their objecthood, their total independence of illusion. Haberle here uses the same device, but for the purpose of *heightening* illusion by means of thingness or objecthood. Parallels between Harnett, Peto, and modern artists are often drawn, but it takes John Haberle to parallel the moderns by turning them inside out.

77

78

79 John Haberle, *Grandma's Hearthstone*, 1890. Oil on canvas, 96×66.
The Detroit Institute of Arts
(Gift of C. W. Churchill in memory of his father).

This tribute to the American Dream is probably the largest *trompe l'œil* painting ever produced in America. It was painted to order for James T. Abbe, a paper tycoon of Northampton, who tore the fireplace and a good part of the wall out of an old Massachusetts farmhouse and had them transported to Haberle's studio in New Haven to serve as the model for this work.

The upper part of the painting—the mantel shelf and the flat overmantel, with their varied *dramatis personae* of objects—is more effective than the lower part, in which the subject requires Haberle to attempt the two things that especially do not lend themselves to *trompe l'œil*: deep space and lively activity (in the flames). Nevertheless, although the fire is relatively unconvincing, "It Fooled the Cat," to quote the headline on an article published in the New Haven *Leader* in 1893; according to this tale, a cat curled up, purred, and went to sleep before the picture as if it were a real fireplace. This, of course, is nothing more than the story of the birds of Zeuxis pecking at the grapes, in one of its protean forms.

We have already noted another form which this ancient folktale often takes in America: Painter of dollar bills is arrested for counterfeiting. Still other forms are as follows:

Student paints coat hook on wall of studio. Old professor tries to hang coat on hook. Told of William Merritt Chase in Katherine M. Roof's biography of that artist; also attributed to Harnett in a version told the writer by a New York art dealer.

Painter's jealous wife tries to push aside sheet in studio behind which she sees nude girl. Discovers both are painted. Told of Mrs. Raphaelle Peale in connection with that artist's *After the Bath*, despite the fact that the painting in question is twenty-nine inches high and the figure of the girl is not more than two feet tall.

Painter paints gold coin on top of bar. Barflies try to pick it up. Told of Jefferson David Chalfant in his family folklore, and of many lesser still-life painters as well.

Dog tries to eat meat on painted sign. Told of the early nineteenth-century artisan painter John A. Woodside by Virgil Barker in his classic book, *American Painting*. Barker adds: "Those who started this story and kept it going, either as an expression of admiration for the sign or as amusing in its own right, were telling more about themselves that about the painter or the dog. They were reiterating one of the major notes in all American interest in painting, and they were also (probably unawares) affirming that Americans were steady in the broadly human tradition coming down from Greece through Rome and Renaissance Italy and nearer England."

79

80 John Haberle, *The Clay Pipe*, (1889). Oil on canvas, $18 \times 8^3/_4$.
Collection Wilbur C. Munnecke, Leland, Michigan.

Trompe l'œil is seldom associated with elegance. As we point out in our Foreword, it is more likely to be associated with general mess and confusion than with anything as orderly and uncluttered as this supremely simple work.

81 John Haberle, *A Dishpan of Flowers*, (1895). Oil on canvas, 20×36.
Courtesy of Kennedy Galleries, Inc., New York.

Haberle began to have trouble with his eyes in the middle '90's. His output dropped precipitately and eventually it ceased altogether. Among his last works are a few still lifes of flowers, like this one, done in a brilliantly colored, shimmering, impressionistic manner. Haberle said he painted in this way because his eyes could no longer endure the strain placed upon them by his efforts to fool the eyes of others, but there may well have been another motivation for the change in style.

Flowers are not good subjects for *trompe l'œil*; Harnett will occasionally paint an isolated bud, but Peto avoids the subject entirely. To the student of American *trompe l'œil* the most unusual thing about *Grandma's Hearthstone* is the bouquet in the vase on the mantel. *Trompe l'œil* needs more solid and tactilely perceptible forms than those of blossoms, and its approach robs them of their fragility and freshness. Flowers need impressionism, and it is no accident that Haberle chooses this subject for his rare excursions into that style

80

81

82   John Haberle, *Night*, (1909). Oil on canvas, 79 × 52.
New Britain Museum of American Art, New Britain, Connecticut
(Gift of Mr. and Mrs. Victor Demmer).

Night was apparently Haberle's last caper, and it may well be his greatest work. It came to light only recently, and this will be its first appearance in a national show.

As we have pointed out earlier, in connection with *Torn in Transit* and *Clock*, one of Haberle's best inventions is the use of paintings which are not in *trompe l'œil* style as *trompe l'œil* objects in *trompe l'œil* settings. Here he carries the diabolical paradox one step further, to its grand finale.

The trick is to make you think, on encountering this picture for the first time, that it has not been completed. Then you suddenly realize that this is not the case at all: it is a completely finished picture of an unfinished picture. The *œil* has been *trompe*'d twice in a row.

This interpretation is validated by several things, including the fact that the canvas is signed and dated. The outlines of the figure and the lightly indicated grid across its upper part, intended to suggest the transfer lines of a squared-off drawing, are in paint, not charcoal, and so are the guide lines for the niche. The female figure is four and a half feet tall, which is just the right size to maintain the idea in proper, precarious balance. As an outline drawing she is far more convincing, from the *trompe l'œil* point of view, than a completed painting of a human being or a statue could possibly be. As we have pointed out

in the Foreword to this catalogue, the human figure does not lend itself well to *trompe l'œil*; nor does its full-scale counterfeit in marble or bronze. When painters of Haberle's persuasion turn to the human figure, they always represent it as a photograph, a chromo, or some kind of engraving. The sketch in *Night*, however big it may be, belongs with those simulated photographs and prints. (If this is "the dehumanization of art," make the most of it.)

The *trompe l'œil* setting for the figure involves tall mosaic panels on both sides, but the one on the right is almost completely covered by a gathered velvet drape (perhaps the most beautifully painted velvet drape in the entire history of the world). The helmet of the knight at the top of the mosaic panel on the left is apparently an outrageous pun on the title of the picture. Below it is a phoenix surrounded by a sundial. The quotation on the scroll at the bottom is from Alexander Pope's epitaph for Sir Isaac Newton. (For this information we thank Charles B. Ferguson, Director of the New Britain Museum of American Art.)

The candles on the shelf at the top of the painting and in the lantern hanging before the figure have burned down and gone out. Could the mysterious spots of diffused or reflected light to be seen at three points in the niche be intended to suggest approaching day?

82

83   Richard LaBarre Goodwin, *Hunting Cabin Door*, n.d. Oil on canvas, 52 × 32.
      Graham Gallery, New York.

84   Richard LaBarre Goodwin, *Hunting Cabin Door*, n.d. Oil on canvas, 55¹/₂ × 34.
      Hirschl and Adler Galleries, Inc., New York.

85   Richard LaBarre Goodwin, *Theodore Roosevelt's Cabin Door*, (ca. 1905).
      Oil on canvas, 21 × 12. Lent by the Vassar College Art Gallery,
      Suzette Morton Davidson Fund, Poughkeepsie, New York.

If Peto is the master of the rack picture and Harnett the master of the tabletop, Goodwin is the master of the hunting-cabin door, of which he painted dozens of examples. All of them were done after 1886, when Harnett's *After the Hunt* made its enormous hit at Theodore Stewart's saloon in New York and created a demand for similar pictures. The punched-in soft hat, which appears in many of these paintings, proclaims their indebtedness to *After the Hunt*; but there are also striking differences. Harnett's rich, green door has huge, magnificent, rusty hinges and a brass key plate in the form of an ancient warrior; Goodwin's doors are plain, battered, unpainted things, with the most unpretentious kind of mail-order hardware. Harnett's gun is a rare, carved, and pearl-inlaid museum piece, carefully dated on its stock, "Trient, 1740"; Goodwin's guns are businesslike modern instruments for killing ducks. Harnett makes much of a grandiose old hunting horn; Goodwin gives us a little pocket whistle instead. Harnett places an ivory-handled sword in his assemblage; Goodwin often rests a pair of old shoes against the door. One might add that Harnett never hunted for anything deadlier than a paintbrush in his life, but Goodwin was an outdoors man and a wanderer—but of that, more later.

Goodwin had a way of preparing for his large cabin-door pictures by painting small, complete pilot versions of them, and these small ones are especially interesting; they are *trompe l'œil* through the wrong end of a telescope. The small Goodwin of the present show, catalogue #85, is the preliminary study for the most celebrated painting of the artist's life.

Goodwin was in Portland, Oregon, in 1905, when there was a fair in that city to commemorate the hundredth anniversary of the Lewis and Clark expedition. One of the exhibits on the fairgrounds was the door of a cabin in which Theodore Roosevelt had lived when he was ranching in the Dakotas in 1890. It was a cabin door like any other; Goodwin had painted dozens like it, and he proceeded to use it as model for a still life in his usual style. Some citizens of Portland wanted to present this painting to T. R. himself, but the chairman of the committee appointed to raise the necessary $2,500 died suddenly before the transaction was completed. He had kept no books, no one knew how much money had been collected or where it was, and so the whole thing fell through. The story of this happening has entered the folklore of American art. It is told about all manner of painters. If one were to stack up all the pictures putatively intended as gifts for Theodore Roosevelt

83

84

but undelivered because of financial difficulties, they would cover the White House, if not the Washington Monument.

Richard LaBarre Goodwin was born in Albany, New York, the son of Edwin Weyburn Goodwin, who devoted his life to painting portraits of the political notables of New York State and left an appalling list of 806 such pictures he had created over the years. Richard Goodwin studied in New York, served in the Civil War, and spent a quarter of a century as an itinerant portrait painter in western New York. Later he lived in Washington, Chicago, Colorado Springs, and along the Pacific Coast. He died in Orange, New Jersey.

85

86   Alexander Pope, *Emblems of the Civil War*, 1888. Oil on canvas, 51 × 54.
Brooklyn Museum, Brooklyn, New York: Dick S. Ramsay Fund.

Pope was a society painter of the back-slapping, club-going variety who spent his entire life in and around Boston. He had an enormous clientele in the right places—even the Czar owned a painting by him—but as is often the case with artists of this kind, his name and work were totally forgotten after his death. He was revived by the present writer in the course of his investigations of Harnett and his school.

Pope did all kinds of painting and a good deal of sculpture as well, but his society people, society dogs, and society horses are best left undisturbed. His variations on *After the Hunt*, however, are extremely interesting. Harnett's iconography of antlers, hat, powder horn, key, canteen, gun, sword, pistol, game bag, and all the rest of it is paraphrased by Pope in numerous highly inventive ways.

According to Donelson F. Hoopes, who wrote an article on Pope for the Brooklyn Museum Annual at the time *Emblems of the Civil War* was acquired (1966), the picture was painted in memory of Major General William Badger Tibbits of Albany. The finding of this picture makes it possible for the writer to correct a ludicrous error in his book, *After the Hunt*. Long before *Emblems of the Civil War* came on the market or was known to survive, I had seen a photograph of it. The large, inverted V-shape in the middle, which is clearly a battle standard sagging between the antlers, looked in that photograph precisely like a pair of pants and is so described in the book.

86

87 Alexander Pope, *Do Not Feed*, n.d. Oil on canvas, $22 \times 27^1/_4$.
Collection Amanda K. Berls, Amagansett, New York.

Pope did innumerable paintings of animals, dead and alive. Strictly speaking, only dead animals belong in a still-life show, but an exception must be made for Pope's pictures of live animals in crates covered with chicken wire. There seem to be a good many of these—dogs, a rooster, rabbits, monkeys. They belong in this exhibition because they are *trompe l'œil* pulled inside out.

Orthodox *trompe l'œil*, as in Pope's *Trumpeter Swan* (#88 in the present catalogue) involves a dead animal spread out on a wall that stops the eye at the picture plane, while the animal itself protrudes into the spectator's space. *Do Not Feed*, and all the paintings that belong with it, precisely reverse this procedure. The sides of the crate and the chicken wire very firmly establish the picture plane in the orthodox fashion, but the animals are *behind* it in a clearly defined area. And since the *trompe l'œil* technique of the dead-animal still life is now completely turned around, the status of the animals is reversed, too. They are now alive instead of dead.

88 Alexander Pope, *The Trumpeter Swan*, 1900. Oil on canvas, $57 \times 44^1/_2$.
Collection Mr. and Mrs. J. William Middendorf II, New York.

According to Hoopes, Pope took a great interest in the conservation of wildlife, and this painting may therefore be interpreted as a reproach to a nation which permitted the trumpeter swan to be slaughtered into near-extinction. The picture hung for many years in the headquarters of the Massachusetts Society for the Prevention of Cruelty to Animals.

87

88

89   Edwin Romanzo Elmer, *Magic Glasses*, n.d. Oil on canvas, $14 \times 10^1/_2$. (Not in exhibition.)
Shelburne Museum, Shelburne, Vermont.

Although this work is not available for our show, it is so charming and so distinguished an example of the tradition with which we are concerned that we are including it in the catalogue.

Edwin Romanzo Elmer spent his entire life in Ashfield, Massachusetts. He was a many-sided, highly creative person who invented machines for making whip-snaps, for shingling houses, and for other purposes, and who painted portraits, genre, and still life throughout his career. In the 1890's he spent a year or two studying painting at the National Academy of Design, but this did not destroy the naïve charm of his work; on the contrary, it made it possible for him to get to the heart of things more directly than before because of greater assurance in technique.

Magic Glasses is probably unique in the entire history of still life. It represents a magnifying glass set in the mouth of a glass vase on the top of a marble table. The polished magnifier reflects the landscape seen through two windows behind the spectator's back. The view through each window is bent and distorted by the convex surface, and one of them is inverted as well.

Similarly distorted exterior and interior scenes as reflected in drinking glasses, crystal balls, and curved metal surfaces are, of course, exceedingly common in Dutch and Flemish genre from the fifteenth century onward, but one would be hard put to find another American example of this device. Even among the Dutch, the reflected image is usually verified, not to say identified, by its repetition in large elsewhere on the canvas. To present the reflected image of a scene entirely outside the spectator's line of vision is unusual. To present two such images is even more unusual, and to turn one of them upside down is, in all probability, unprecedented.

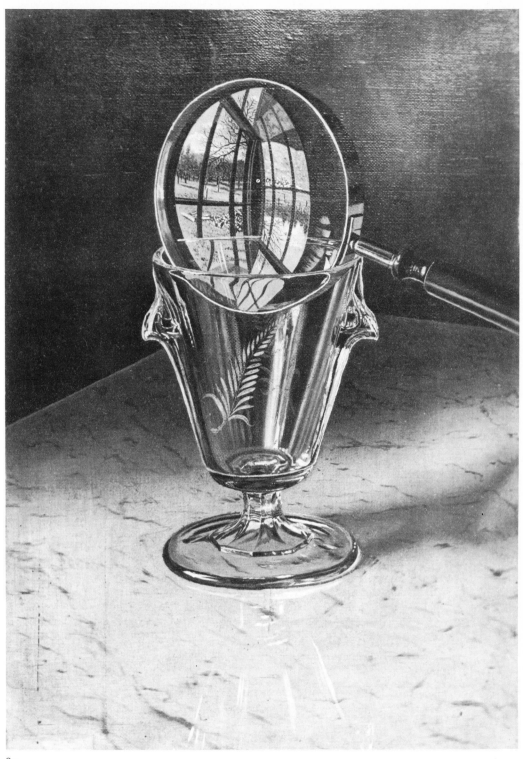

89

JOSEPH DECKER
1853–1920

90   Joseph Decker, *Russet Apples on a Bough,* (ca. 1880). Oil on canvas, $17^1/_4 \times 27^1/_2$.
Collection H. John Heinz, Pittsburgh, Pennsylvania.

91   Joseph Decker, *Their Winter Hoard,* (ca. 1890). Oil on canvas, 11×17.
Collection Mr. and Mrs. Ferdinand H. Davis, New York.

Joseph Decker was born in Germany, came to the United States at the age of fourteen, studied at the National Academy of Design, and apparently lived all the rest of his life in Brooklyn. There he painted "landscapes, cattle, still life, and portraits"; so his work is described in the manuscript catalogue of the Thomas B. Clarke Collection at the Whitney Museum of American Art. His still lifes, in an immaculatistic style worthy of a Charles Sheeler, seem to have been done very early in his career. Later he fell under the influence of George Inness, and his cows and pastures are unrecognizable as products of the same hand. In *After the Hunt* it is even suggested that there may have been two different Joseph Deckers working in Brooklyn at the same time, but recent research has shown this fine theory to be untenable.

90

91

WILLIAM KEANE
Dates of birth and death unknown

92 William Keane, *Still Life with Banjo*, (ca. 1889). Oil on canvas, 40 × 25.
California Palace of the Legion of Honor, San Francisco.

Nothing is known about William Keane beyond the fact that four paintings bearing his name have come to light in the Philadelphia-Camden area. Two of them are still lifes with upside-down banjos; but the other one of this type has only a horseshoe and a newspaper clipping in addition to the musical instrument.

The present work looks like a Haberlean parody of Harnett, with special reference to the hats of *After the Hunt* and his still lifes of violins and sheet music. Keane's music bears the copyright date "mdccclxxxix," which upon being translated into Arabic seems to work out as 1889.

92

93   Claude Raguet Hirst, *An Interesting Book*, (ca. 1890). Watercolor on paper, 10 × 14¹/₂.
Collection Mr. Francis Hutchens, San Francisco.

94   Claude Raguet Hirst, *Still Life*, (ca. 1890). Watercolor on paper, 10 × 14¹/₂.
The Butler Institute of American Art, Youngstown, Ohio.

Claude Raguet Hirst is the only habitual painter in watercolors among those in the present show; despite her first name, she is also the only lady. Miss Hirst's record at the National Academy of Design shows that she painted still lifes of flowers and fruit until 1890; then she took up the tabletop still life with the pipe and books, and specialized in it for many years. Throughout the 1880's and well into the 1890's, Miss Hirst's studio was at 30 East 14th Street in New York. From 1886 until 1889, Harnett had a studio next door, at 28 East 14th. The reason for Miss Hirst's switch to the pipe and book seems clear.

93

94

VICTOR DUBREUIL
Dates of birth and death unknown

95   Victor Dubreuil, *Don't Make a Move!*, (1900). Oil on canvas, 24 × 32.
    Courtesy of Kennedy Galleries, Inc., New York.

Very little is known about Dubreuil beyond the fact that in the 1890's he frequented a saloon known as Dickens House at 38th Street and Seventh Avenue in New York. He traded some of his pictures for food and drink there, and some of these pictures, which have survived, contain letters addressed to the artist on West 43rd and West 44th Streets. For at least some time, then, he drifted about the Times Square neighborhood.

He was obsessed with money, doubtless because he never had any. There is also a remarkable vein of brutality in his work, and these two things come together here in a veritable *Bonnie and Clyde*. Strictly speaking this is not a *trompe l'œil* painting, because the figures are smaller than the scale of life, but *trompe l'œil* devices are used throughout. The teller's cage serves as the optical backstop. The book, the drawer, "Bonnie's" hand, and the newspaper come forward in *trompe l'œil* fashion, and the figures stand in a kind of negative *trompe l'œil* space, like the dogs in catalogue #87 above. The totally flat and totally unrealistic newspaper observes the tradition most faithfully. Look closely at its dateline.

96   Victor Dubreuil, *The Safe*, n.d. Oil on canvas, 30 × 25.
    Courtesy of Kennedy Galleries, Inc., New York.

As is pointed out in the note on catalogue #95, Dubreuil was obsessed with money. He painted it in every conceivable way. Barrels of money were a favorite theme of his; also piles, stacks, garlands, and nosegays of money. He does not often tell us precisely how much his picture is worth as hard and soft cash, but the accounting here shows that the North, South, East, and West Railroad possessed exactly $492,302,000 in bank notes and $90,296.50 in gold and silver coins. That the picture is also a Mondrianesque abstraction in rectangles may be accidental, but this does not make the rectangles any the less rectangular.

95

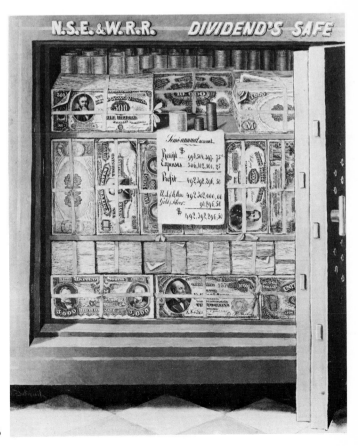

96

97   Victor Dubreuil, *Declaration of War*, (1898). Oil on canvas, $11^1/_2 \times 10$.
Noah Goldowsky Gallery, New York.

For all their delight in newspapers, the American *trompe l'œil* painters do not record history or commemorate specific events. This picture is an all but unique exception to that rule. That it commemorates a declaration of war underlines what is said above about the vein of brutality running through Dubreuil's work.

F. DANTON, JR.
Dates of birth and death unknown

98   F. Danton, Jr., *Time Is Money*, 1894. Oil on canvas, $16^{15}/_{16} \times 21^1/_8$.
Wadsworth Atheneum, Hartford, Connecticut:
The Ella Gallup Sumner and Mary Catlin Sumner Collection.

Nothing whatsoever is known about this artist except that he painted a few Dubreuil-like still lifes involving money. This one merits inclusion in a national show because of the trickery of its lower right corner.

The wide wooden frame is painted to continue the grain and the cracks of the door painted on the canvas. The frame projects about a half inch ahead of the canvas on all four sides and therefore casts shadows upon it. At the lower right-hand corner of the frame, at the point where the work is signed, is a square area *painted* with cast shadows to create the illusion that that square is recessed to the same depth as the canvas. It is worth noting, also, that the frame is punctured with nail holes, some real, some painted, and the real nail holes have painted splinters around their rims precisely like those around the rims of the simulated ones.

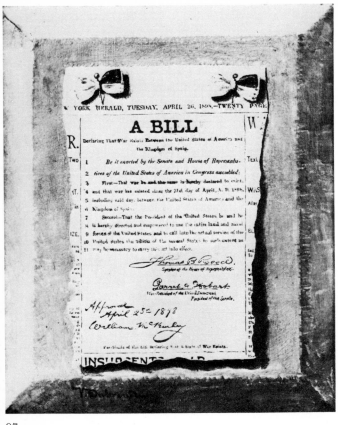

97

98

GEORGE COPE
1855–1929

99   George Cope, *The Day's Bag*, 1910. Oil on canvas, $21^1/_2 \times 16^1/_4$.
Collection Amanda K. Berls, Amagansett, New York.

George Cope spent his entire life in West Chester, Pennsylvania, and innumerable still lifes by him are still cherished in the homes of that city. His style is a little naïve, although the subject in this case tends to conceal that fact. Hanging-game pictures are the commonest of all still lifes, especially by amateur painters; this one, however, is an imitation of a Harnett now in the National Gallery of Canada.

JEFFERSON DAVID CHALFANT
1856–1931

100   Jefferson David Chalfant, *Violin and Bow*, 1889. Oil on canvas, $36 \times 21^1/_2$.
Lent by The Metropolitan Museum of Art, George A. Hearn Fund, 1966.

Jefferson David Chalfant lived in Wilmington, Delaware, most of his life. He painted portraits, genre, and everything else that could be painted, but he is most memorable for his still lifes which, in almost every instance, can be traced to a prototype by Harnett. His reliance on the older artist, however, does not detract from Chalfant's exqui-site craftsmanship. Chalfant usually simplifies Harnett's composition, as will be made dramatic if one compares this work with catalogue #52 above: no doors, no hinges, no sheet music, no horseshoes, no piccolos, no locks or cards; just beautiful painting of a violin and bow.

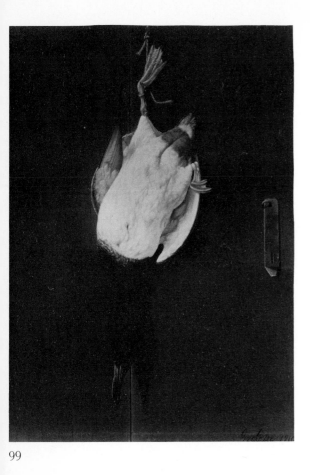

99

100

CHARLES MEURER
1865–1955

101 Charles Meurer, *Doughboy's Equipment*, 1921. Oil on canvas, 68 × 40.
The Butler Institute of American Art, Youngstown, Ohio.

Charles Meurer spent most of his life in Terrace Park, Ohio, a suburb of Cincinnati. He was the last living member of the great school of American *trompe l'œil* painters; like the last-ditch representatives of most great traditions, his ultimate style is an unconscious caricature of everything the tra-dition stood for. But his attempt to adapt the theme of Harnett's *After the Hunt* to the military accouterments of World War I is interesting, especially now that World War I is taking on romantic, historic overtones.

HENRY ALEXANDER
1862–1895

102 Henry Alexander, *The Laboratory of Thomas Price*, (ca. 1887). Oil on canvas, 36 × 30.
Lent by The Metropolitan Museum of Art, Punnett Fund, 1939.

Alexander was born in San Francisco, was trained in Munich, and practiced in his native city and in New York. He died at the age of thirty-three. In 1906 his family assembled many of his works for a memorial exhibition in San Francisco, and they were all destroyed in the famous earthquake and fire of that year. In view of the brevity of his life and the disaster that overtook so much of his output, it is amazing that so many of his works can still be found.

Alexander invented a very special kind of still life, apart from the *trompe l'œil* tradition, but somehow related to it. He loved to paint pictures of people using large quantities of equipment of different sizes and shapes, all of which he studies very carefully and usually paints more convincingly than he does the people. He does bearded gentlemen playing chess in offices cluttered with pens, inkstands, ledgers, safes, and so on; he did a cobbler's shop with endless lasts on shelves and a taxidermist's shop with its tools and an amazing scatter of dead animals in every conceivable stage of mounting. His best works, however, are his several studies of the laboratory of Thomas Price, the California state mineralogist and assayer, and the infinite shapes and colors provided by its chemical glassware and its contents. Note also how successfully Alexander counterpoints the curvilinear forms of Price's bottles and retorts against the rectangles of windows, shelves, and tables.

101

102

MILNE RAMSEY
1846–1915

103   Milne Ramsey, *Still Life*, 1911. Oil on canvas, 31 × 25.
Collection Dr. Kenneth C. Slagle, West Chester, Pennsylvania.

Milne Ramsey lived in Philadelphia all through the Harnett-Peto era, occasionally genuflected toward those younger artists in his subject matter, but firmly maintained his own style so far as the rendition of textures and other surface effects is concerned. The tumblers in this painting go back to John F. Francis; the ambiguous handling of the surface of the table recalls Peto; but the modeling of the pitcher, with its dominating assurance and authority, recalls no one in the *trompe l'œil* tradition. The radiant color, too, is very much Ramsey's own.

WILLIAM HENRY YATES
1845–1934

104   William Henry Yates, *Still Life with Window*, 1908. Oil on board, $41^3/_4 \times 26^1/_2$.
Hirschl and Adler Galleries, Inc., New York.

The entire literature on Yates seems to consist of a single paragraph in an article on the collection of James Brown in *The Magazine Antiques* for November 1963. It says that he lived in Auburn, New York, where he painted "local views, sweeping Western panoramas, scenes of New York City, and a *Battle of Gettysburg* bought by the 1881 encampment of the Grand Army of the Republic and presented to the Soldiers' Home in Bath, New York, in that year." All of which does nothing to explain how he managed so astonishingly to predict Andrew Wyeth in this work.

JEFFERSON DAVID CHALFANT
(see above)

105   Jefferson David Chalfant, *Which Is Which?*, n.d.
Oil and postage stamp on enameled copper, 5 × 7.
Collection Ernest Jarvis, Fort Lauderdale, Florida.

Chalfant pastes a real two-cent stamp next to a painted one and, with a painted newspaper clipping beneath, challenges the beholder to tell the difference. In the eighty-odd years since this was done, the real stamp has faded until it is almost illegible. The painted counterfeit is as good today as it was on the day that Chalfant put it there. On which note we lower the curtain on *The Reality of Appearance*.

104

103

105

uine. Mr. Chalfant proposes to paste a real stamp on the canvas beside his painting, and the puzzling question will be "Which is which?"

LENDERS TO THE EXHIBITION

Mr. and Mrs. James W. Alsdorf, Winnetka, Illinois; Mrs. John Barnes, New York; Amanda K. Berls, Amagansett, New York; Mrs. Mimi David Bloch, New York; Dick Button, New York; Mr. and Mrs. Ferdinand H. Davis, New York; Mr. and Mrs. Alfred Frankenstein, San Francisco; Mr. and Mrs. Morton Funger, Chevy Chase, Maryland; Mr. and Mrs. John L. Gardner, Hamilton, Massachusetts; Mr. and Mrs. Robert C. Graham, New York; Mrs. Harold H. Hays, Philadelphia; H. John Heinz, Pittsburgh, Pennsylvania; Francis Hutchens, San Francisco; Ernest Jarvis, Fort Lauderdale, Florida; Barbara B. Lassiter, Winston-Salem, North Carolina; Dr. and Mrs. Irving Levitt, Southfield, Michigan; Dr. and Mrs. John J. McDonough, Youngstown, Ohio; Mr. and Mrs. J. William Middendorf II, New York; Wilbur C. Munnecke, Leland, Michigan; Mr. and Mrs. Jess Pavey, Birmingham, Michigan; Mr. and Mrs. Marvin Preston, Ferndale, Michigan; Mr. and Mrs. Cresson Pugh, Mamaroneck, New York; William Selnick, New York; Dr. Kenneth C. Slagle, West Chester, Pennsylvania; Mrs. Mollie D. Snyder, Philadelphia; Mr. and Mrs. Mortimer Spiller, Buffalo, New York; Mr. and Mrs. Donald S. Stralem, New York; Paul Zuckerman, Franklin, Michigan.

Amon Carter Museum of Western Art, Fort Worth, Texas; Brooklyn Museum, Brooklyn, New York; The Butler Institute of American Art, Youngstown, Ohio; California Palace of the Legion of Honor, San Francisco; City Art Museum of Saint Louis, St. Louis, Missouri; The Cleveland Museum of Art, Cleveland, Ohio; Dallas Museum of Fine Arts, Dallas, Texas; The Detroit Institute of Fine Arts, Detroit, Michigan; Gallery of Fine Arts, Columbus, Ohio; Graves Art Gallery, Sheffield, England; Historical Society of Pennsylvania, Philadelphia; M. H. de Young Memorial Museum, San Francisco; The Metropolitan Museum of Art, New York; Milwaukee Art Center, Milwaukee, Wisconsin; Munson-Williams-Proctor Institute, Utica, New York; Museum of Art, Carnegie Institute, Pittsburgh, Pennsylvania; Museum of Fine Arts, Springfield, Massachusetts; The Museum of Modern Art, New York; The Newark Museum, Newark, New Jersey; New Britain Museum of American Art, New Britain, Connecticut; Onondaga Historical Association, Syracuse, New York; Philadelphia Museum of Art, Philadelphia; The Phillips Collection, Washington, D.C.; The Reading Public Museum and Art Gallery, Reading, Pennsylvania; Reynolda House, Winston-Salem, North Carolina; Santa Barbara Museum of Art; Shelburne Museum, Shelburne, Vermont; Suffolk Museum and Carriage House, Stony Brook, New York; University of Massachusetts Art Gallery, Amherst, Massachusetts; Vassar College Art Gallery, Poughkeepsie, New York; Wadsworth Atheneum, Hartford, Connecticut.

Noah Goldowsky Gallery, New York; Graham Gallery, New York; Hirschl and Adler Galleries, Inc., New York; Kennedy Galleries, Inc., New York.

106.   William M. Harnett, *Latakia II,* 1880. Oil on canvas, 11 × 15. Collection Mr. and Mrs. Mortimer Spiller, Buffalo, New York.

ASTLEY DAVID MONTAGUE COOPER
1856–1924

107.   A. D. M. Cooper, *A Salute to Buffalo Bill,* 1904. Oil on canvas, 50 × 40. Collection Mr. and Mrs. Walter Hochschild, Blue Mountain Lake, New York.

Astley David Montague Cooper specialized in Wild West subjects of various kinds: portraits of Indians, scenes of buffalo hunting, of Indian battles, and so on. He also did large, panoramic, neo-classical pictures, and painted an enormous still life recording Mrs. Leland Stanford's jewel collection just before it was sold to provide funds for the Stanford University Library. Cooper was born in St. Louis and started his career in Colorado, but spent most of his life in San Jose, California. Without much question, his most celebrated work is the *trompe l'œil* tribute to Buffalo Bill which hung for many years on the grand staircase of the Hotel Irma in Buffalo Bill's town of Cody, Wyoming, and is now in the collection of the Buffalo Bill Historical Center in that city. Our painting, however, is almost identical with that one.

Printed in the Netherlands